CW00434937

LESSONS
FROM THE
FISH

LESSONS
FROM THE
FISH

**An Anthology of Fishing Experiences
written by National Celebrities**

Selected, edited, and with an introduction by

Len Colclough

Illustrations by
Terence Lambert

To Benefit
SECOND CHANCE
A Charity for children who need special help
Greytown House
130/136 Elm Grove
Southsea
Hampshire
PO5 1LR

SWAN·HILL
PRESS

ILLUSTRATIONS
by Terence Lambert

A limited edition signed and numbered colour print of the cover illustration is available from Second Chance, Greytown House 130/136 Elm Grove, Southsea, Hampshire, PO5 1LR. Composite limited edition prints of the black and white illustrations are also available.

Second Chance is extremely grateful to Terence Lambert for his generous gift of this exceptional and much sought-after work.

Copyright © 1996 The Second Chance Charity
First published in the UK in 1996 by Swan Hill Press, an imprint of Airlife Publishing Ltd

British Library Cataloguing in Publication Data
A catalogue record for this book is available from the British Library

ISBN 1 85310 818 9

Typeset by Hewer Text Composition Services, Edinburgh
Printed in England by Biddles Ltd, Guildford and King's Lynn

Swan Hill Press
an imprint of Airlife Publishing Ltd
101 Longden Road, Shrewsbury, SY3 9EB, England.

Contents

Acknowledgements

Second Chance, the charity for children who need special help, wishes to thank the following writers who have provided new and previously unpublished material for this anthology:

Bernard Aldrich, Fiona Armstrong, Keith Arthur, John Bailey, Dr Bruno Broughton, Brian Clarke, Len Colclough, Chris Dawn, Ted Entwhistle, Tom Fort, John and Llin Golding MP, Douglas Hulme, Martin James, Peter Lapsley, Lord Mason of Barnsley, Sir Cranley Onslow, Tim Paisley, Geoffrey Palmer, Tony Pawson, Peter Peck, David Profumo, Anton Rodgers, Frances Shand Kydd, Sir Geoffrey Johnson Smith, Sir David Steel, Trevor Stewart, Peter Stone and Jim Whippy.

The editor and Second Chance also wish to thank the following writers, publishers and literary representatives for their permissions to use copyright material:

Tales of a Water Bailiff by Bob Davison, from which two extracts are taken, is published under the Swan Hill Press imprint by Airlife Publishing Ltd.

'Instinct' by Francis T. Grant is from *Salmon Flyfishing, The Dynamics Approach*, published by Airlife Publishing Ltd under the Swan Hill Press imprint.

The extract from *Hansard*, the official report of the House of Commons, which appears in John and Llin Golding MP's piece 'The Boat is the Enemy' comes from the debate on the Activity Centres (Young Persons' Safety) Bill published on 1 March 1995, and is Parliamentary copyright.

'Small Stuff and Beginners, is Chapter IV of *Fishing for a Year* by Jack Hargreaves, first published in 1951, reproduced by courtesy of the Medlar Press, Ellesmere, Shropshire, England.

'The Emperor's Breakfast' and 'Fishing for Salmon' are reprinted by permission of Scribner, a division of Simon & Schuster from *A Trout and Salmon Fisherman for Seventy-Five Years* by Edward R. Hewitt. Copyright © 1948 by Charles Scribner's Sons, renewed.

The two extracts from *A Summer on the Test* by John Waller Hills are reproduced by kind permission of the publishers, André Deutsch Ltd.

'The Fellow-Feeling' by A.A. Luce is from *Fishing and Thinking*, published under the Swan Hill Press imprint by Airlife Publishing Ltd.

'A Game Of Nods' is from *In the Ring of the Rise* by Vincent C. Marinaro, published by Airlife Publishing Ltd in the UK. Copyright © 1976 by Vincent Marinaro and reprinted by permission of Lyons & Burford, Publishers, New York.

The George Melly piece 'There's More Than One Rise' is an edited extract from *Mellymobile*, and appears by kind permission of Robson Books Ltd.

'Nature Watch' comprises extracts from *Tails and the Unexpected* by Billee Chapman Pincher, published under the Swan Hill Press imprint by Airlife Publishing Ltd.

'Can Fish Communicate?' by Mary M. Pratt first appeared in *Better Angling Through Simple Science* and is reproduced by kind permission of Fishing News Books, part of Blackwell Science Ltd.

Datus Proper's 'Conversations With Trout' were first recorded in the book of that name published by Airlife Publishing Ltd under the Swan Hill Press imprint.

The two chapters by Arthur Ransome, 'Carp' and 'Fishing in Books and Fishing in Fact', are from *Rod and Line* and are reprinted by permission of the Arthur Ransome Estate and Dan Franklin of Jonathan Cape.

Reg Righyni's piece 'By Night For Sea Trout?' appears in *Fishing Reflections* published under the Swan Hill Press imprint by Airlife Publishing Ltd.

'An Angry Birth' by Donald V. Roberts is an extract from *Nymph Fishing Lakes* and is reproduced by kind permission of Frank Amato Publications, Portland, Oregon.

Dave Whitlock's 'How Trout Feed' is taken from *A Guide to Aquatic Trout Food*, published under the Swan Hill Press imprint by Airlife Publishing Ltd.

'The Trout's World' is copyright 1986 by Lee Wulff and is reprinted from *Trout on a Fly* by permission of Lyons & Burford, Publishers, New York.

'Camouflage' and 'Dry Fly Fishing for Salmon' by Major Ashley-Dodd first appeared in *A Fisherman's Log* published by Constable in 1929. The copyright owner is untraceable despite the charity's efforts through ex-service organisations and Major Ashley-Dodd's last known address. Second Chance would welcome news from anyone claiming copyright.

Finally, a word of thanks to Audrey James for her speedy and efficient typing of much of the text, to Gordon Wigginton (a great angler) of The Angel Hotel, Guildford, for the use of his office equipment on the frequent occasions when the charity's elderly and overused computer and copier facilities broke down and to Roy Eveleigh for reading the proofs.

Len Colclough

Introduction

It was in 1942, around the time of my thirteenth birthday, that I discovered the wondrous joys of fishing. A raspberry cane discarded by a 'Digging for Victory' neighbour, 2 yards of black sewing thread, a pin bent into a V for a hook, all tied together with clumsy knots – this was the complete outfit I carried a little fearfully to the side of an old mill pond. Occasionally, I had seen other boys fishing there, sometimes even old men, but today I had the pond to myself. The mill too, for that matter, for lack of work had closed it down even before the war.

I knew of no bait other than the worm and so I dug my heel into the hard ground where no self-respecting worm would have ventured to blunt its nose and, after ruining one shoe, I tried pulling up clumps of grass by the roots. One tiny blue-veined crawler was exposed and, after many rehearsals, was persuaded to pose on the bent pin, though not for long. As I swung the cane over the dark, deep water I noted with dismay how the hook landed in one place while the worm splashed down in another. My first experience with a barbless hook had taught me the joys of groundbaiting, at least.

Another worm, better secured, was taken and lost almost as soon as it hit the water only a yard from the bank. Excitement and wonder filled me as I ruined my other shoe kicking for worms, but soon I was fishing again with an anticipation that almost hurt. All my attention battled against the glinting curtain that was the surface film, shielding the activity below from my youthful need to see the biggest fish in the pond slowly, majestically, approaching the bait whose wriggling obscured the sharp steely point that was to lift him from his watery home and into my hands. And it happened!

Of course I remember well that first fish, those few ounces of primaeval life in the palm of my hand, life from another world, albeit one of murk and mud. More, much more than that, I recall an excitement I did not understand at the time but which I would now describe as the strange reality of passing into another world and looking anew from there at our own world with eyes undimmed by idle familiarity – the sort of excitement that must have triggered Charles Kingsley's thoughts towards *Yeast* and *The Water Babies*.

It is an excitement that knows no boundaries; J. W. Hills must have had an accountant's brain to become Financial Secretary to the Treasury yet his writings about the River Test contain some of the finest prose in English literature and prompted non-angler Virginia Woolf to enquire: 'Is it possible that to remove veils from trees it is necessary to fish? – our conscious mind must be all body, and then the unconscious mind leaps to the top and strips off veils?'

Major Hills had lost his fish, an old male salmon, when he described the few seconds it was on the hook, and afterwards:

> 'The fish went perfectly mad, overran my reel . . . jammed it, and broke my twisted gut trace. It all happened in a few seconds' . . . But they were seconds of extraordinary intensity, seconds lived alone 'in a world of strong emotion, cut off from all else'. And when he looked up all had changed. 'The trees had their bright young leaves, some of them golden, the wild cherry was covered with drifts of snow and the ground was covered with dog mercury, looking as though it had been newly varnished . . . I felt receptive to every sight, every colour and every sound, as though I had walked through a world from which a veil had been withdrawn.'

This arousal of the imagination through fishing has been around for many centuries and has been recognised by writers from Homer to Ted Hughes. The drawing away of the veils described by J. W. Hills and recognised by Virginia Woolf must have been experienced by many who have taken it for themselves, been amused or inspired in a selfish sort of way, and have not tugged aside the veils far enough for others, less fortunate, to see the brightness of the trees. That was left to Douglas Hulme, a teacher at a special school for children with learning difficulties.

Inner-city estates, the appalling rise of the drug culture, the collapse of family life following the years of a permissive society, irresponsible and persuasive media which instruct a young mind that it is fun to mock anyone in authority, threaten teachers, disparage elected politicians, sneer at the Royal Family, and use the courts to undermine the police – all these and more are heavy veils to be stripped away and the special school teacher discovered the way – with angling!

Imagine taking a battered or sexually abused child from a poverty-stricken inner-city area – a child with learning difficulties, a single parent and three or four brothers and sisters – into the countryside, teaching them to fish and thrill to the rod pulling down to the water's surface – another veil, but this one soon torn aside by the fish to give the child a thrill beyond belief. Suddenly with some, slowly with others, comes the realisation that here in nature is something bigger than self, bigger even than a tower block, something the child cannot beat but can work with. And with them is an adult with whom they can interact, perhaps for the first time in their young lives. Someone who cares. Someone with whom they can share confidences which could become a means of helping not only the child but the whole family.

Second Chance is the charity for these children who need special help. Doug Hulme and his helpers, all volunteers, need help too in order to carry on this necessary work, stripping away veils and showing light, letting the children see the brightness of trees, children whose handicaps are hidden inside them, needing understanding, advocacy, employment assistance, and support services of all kinds. Would you care to strip away a veil?

The Duke of Wellington
Foreword

In the fast moving world in which we live, new sports and leisure activities seem to emerge all the time to claim our participation. However, surely there can be none that is more deeply satisfying than the oldest sport of all – fishing with an angle, or angling as it is now known.

All of us who fish become hooked (sometimes physically I am afraid) and we know that our sport is the most therapeutic of all when it comes to countering the stresses of life. I can imagine no therapy which could match angling for meeting the needs of children with special requirements.

Bernard Aldrich

Never Say Never

For forty years I have been involved with fishing as keeper of six miles of the River Test as it flows through the Broadlands Estate in Hampshire. During that time I have become a dedicated salmon fisherman but also I enjoy trout, coarse, and sea fishing. In all that time I have found nature to be a great leveller. Fishing in particular has a way of making us aware that the more we learn, the less we know. Those of us who like to think of ourselves as experts are often taken down a peg or two, just to keep us in our places. What follows is a case in point.

The summer had been long and hot with no rain and the river was very low, with warm, crystal-clear water into which the salmon were not running. They were waiting in the estuary for the much-needed rain to fall.

Two of my very experienced and consistent catchers of salmon had telephoned the previous day to discuss their chances of catching a fish and decided the best time to start was early morning and then again in the cool of late evening. That was the plan!

Next morning they arrived at the crack of dawn, bringing with them their twelve-year-old sons, who were on holiday from school. It was to be a treat for the boys and a good opportunity for them to learn the rudiments of fishing. The two men fished hard, with their sons watching, until ten o'clock. Nothing was caught or even seen as the sun became brassy and the heat intensified. We experts knew it was pointless to continue with any serious fishing and the next hour was spent giving the boys their first lessons in casting. This soon palled in the heat and the two fathers decided to seek sustenance in town and eventually returned with many good things for a picnic lunch. What with the exertions of the morning and the effects of a long, leisurely lunch, the men retired to deckchairs in the shade of the riverside trees. The boys, however, with the energy and enthusiasm of youth, picked up their fathers' rods and went upstream to practise their casting.

At four o'clock tea was ready in the fishing hut and the two lads returned to join us, looking more than a little bit sheepish. Oh, dear, I thought, maybe they have broken one of the rods. I watched apprehensively as they approached their fathers, saying, 'We hope we have done the right thing!' With that they produced two beautiful salmon, one of 8 pounds and one of 10, both beautiful fresh-run fish with sea-lice clinging to their sides.

The boys had hooked their fish under 'impossible' conditions and then, with no experience at all, played the fish right out. Without a landing net they had tailed out the fish by hand and despatched them with a large stone.

Of course we were delighted, amazed, and a little bit miffed that our superior knowledge had proved flawed. My own lesson from that experience is that the only way to catch fish is to keep fishing.

Another 'fact' well known to experienced fishers of salmon is that a fish hooked and lost will seldom, if ever, take the bait again, and certainly not for several days unless the fish moves up a pool or two. I have often seen fish leap from the water having been fished over and have commented, 'That's a pricked fish!'

On one occasion, however, I was out along the river bank visiting my fishermen when I stopped to chat with one of them. Standing close to the water's edge and gazing into the clear water through my Polaroid spectacles I was amazed to see a salmon of about 12 pounds lying less than 2 yards from us, totally undisturbed by our presence. Quietly I explained the situation to the angler who, equally quietly and with hardly a movement, passed me his rod, which was already mounted with a prawn.

Very, very slowly I swung the rod over the water and lowered the prawn down towards the fish, which swam up and took the offering at once. I struck hard and the fish was on. He came to the surface thrashing about, spraying water everywhere – and came off! I retrieved the bait and found that the hook had straightened. Glancing into the river I was surprised to see that the fish had returned immediately to exactly the same position.

I put on a new hook and bait to try the fish again, not expecting him to take. I was hoping to scare him out of the pool, as 'pricked' fish often prevent others from taking. To my utter astonishment the fish took immediately, ran strongly to mid-stream, came to the surface and once more came off! This time I watched the fish drop back, swim in a circle and return again to the same spot.

Hardly believing what was happening, I put on a new hook and bait and presented it to the fish. After a second or two he took it exactly as before, again thrashed about on the surface and once more came off. The new hook, like the others, had straightened out and I fingered it thoughtfully as I watched the salmon repeat his earlier manoeuvre and return to his lie.

I decided to rest the fish for a minute or two while I went back to my Land-Rover for one of my own prawn tackles. I knew these were built with very strong irons and by this time I was a little fed up with the soft wire of the fisherman's own hooks. In the meantime the salmon had returned to his favoured spot and, when I once again lowered the prawn, he quite quickly swam up and took it.

This time there was no mistake! The fish fought hard but the hook held and, after a fierce struggle, he was netted – a beautiful, determined salmon of 11 pounds.

That fish had been hooked and lost in the same spot three times, the hook marks being plainly visible in his mouth, and yet he still took for a fourth time. It was a strange and, for me, unique experience which reinforces the truth drummed into me by my dear old predecessor, the legendary Walter Geary: 'Never say never and never say always' – a very good rule to remember when working with nature and most especially when fishing.

Fiona Armstrong

Fishing On Film

As they say in show business, never work with children or animals. How right they are, particularly when it comes to fish! Heaven knows, to the hopeful angler these trout, salmon and sea trout are unpredictable enough, but to the presenter with an expectant TV crew by her shoulder, they are downright impossible!

And that, I always tell myself, is the first lesson of fishing on film. Do not expect too much. Of course, as an angler I have learned to expect very little and simply to enjoy the moment. But, if I am honest, when I go out I do hope to make some sort of show for the cameras.

Lesson number two is more straightforward. To get the right pictures with the right fish, go to the river when there is a fair chance of catching something. But when that fair chance might be is anybody's guess. Presumably the fish have a better idea than most . . .

You see, the problem with an angling programme is that unless one has days, or better still weeks, to faithfully flog the water, one is definitely under pressure to deliver. For, let us face it, who wants to watch a fishing programme with no fish?

The first time I went out with a crew, I was lucky to get a patient lot. It was a team from Border Television, all good country lads and lasses, folks born and bred in the north, people well used to walking and wading – the sort who did not mind hanging about in the rain and who understood the pace and unpredictability of a life outdoors. They were quite unlike the London boys, bless them, who arrive complaining about the midges and dodging the puddles in their designer wellies. Complete with fast cars and even faster camera shutters, they may well spend the first half-hour on the mobile phone ringing the office. Then, satisfied that there are no bigger and more urgent stories to follow up elsewhere, they cheerfully say that they are ready to shoot the salmon that you, the presenter and angler, are just about to catch.

Two blank days into filming and I too was ready to shoot a salmon, could I only see one! My Border TV crew, though, were still totally supportive. They knew that I could not catch to order and they were prepared to wait. But, let us face it, in fishing there is waiting and there is waiting – especially when one is only watching.

It is in the wee, watching hours that thoughts turn to budgets, schedules and the dreaded overtime. Remarks like, 'I don't want to worry you, but we've only got half an hour of tape left' or 'You do realise, of course, that in ten minutes we'll have lost the light,' are interesting but not exactly helpful when one is desperately changing one's umpteenth fly and crossing one's fingers at the same time.

The problem is that the fish know you are there and they know also that you have a camera. If they are hard to catch at normal times, filming procedures make it well nigh impossible!

For a start, there is the make-up. Yes, the powder and paint, something a fly-fisher should never normally have to concern him- or herself with! It is, of course, important to look as natural as possible by the river. But then again, modern cameras are particularly cruel when it comes to lines and blemishes and it would be a brave presenter – female *or* male – who would dare to appear on screen without a slight dusting of something.

Next, there is the fun of casting a large-hooked fly with a cameraman to the front and a soundman to the rear. I hope I am insured for damaged ears – or worse!

Then there are the retakes, the endless retakes. 'Take 22' may be good for casting practise, but it is not so good when it comes to not disturbing the water . . . Yes, when it comes to fishing on film, the fish win hands down.

But listen to me! For what a joy – to be able to make a hobby a job, to go fishing – and get paid for it! From a remote trout lake on the Isle of Man to the world-famous Junction Pool, from the mouth of the Solway to a country beck, to cast a line with a bishop and a nobleman, a ghillie and a chef – there may be no fish, but this is angling at its best.

At Ladywell on the Tweed, we met the man they call *Mr Tweed*, angling expert and fishing writer Dr Bill Currie. Folk still stop me and comment on the beauty and skill of his spey-casting.

Further on up at majestic Upper Floors, we found the Duke of Roxburghe, who told of his life-long passion for angling; of how he caught his first salmon on a trout rod at the age of eight and carried it proudly home across his bicycle handlebars. He has a lot to live up to, for his grandmother was one of the best flyfishers around, at one time taking sixty salmon off one beat in just a few days. As each fish weighed about 20 pounds, it was no mean achievement. Catches like this go some way to explaining why estate workers in days gone by were wont to complain if they were given salmon to eat more than twice a week! We are not so lucky. We film and we film, but still no fish!

Down in Cumbria we went to the river Eden, to meet a wonderful man who can tie flies with the best of them. Jim McKay is his name, a ghillie-cum-fishing consultant, who created a special one just for me. I chose the colours and he made it up – a red, silver and yellow combination, which we called 'Fiona's Fancy'. It certainly looked the part and I was sure it would attract something, but, alas, on this filming trip, it was not to be christened in the appropriate manner.

'I can't think what's happened,' said Jim as we waded into ever deeper water, casting for all we were worth. 'We were catching them last week,' Yes, and you'll probably catch them next week, I thought rather ungraciously. But never this week, of course! Always jam and salmon tomorrow, never today – that is fishing, and that is filming! And those are lessons from the fish.

I did eventually get something, however, as we crossed the sea to the Isle of Man. 'The Isle of Man?' I hear you say. 'Is there really, good fishing on the Isle of Man?' The answer is, yes! It is mostly lake and reservoir fishing, with a mix of brown trout and rainbows, but there is some river sport too, and Manx salmon are reputedly delicious.

It was the first day of our filming on the island and we arrived in the pouring rain at a small, private lake.

'While we're taking the equipment out of the van, you may as well go to the water and practise with the trout rod,' said the producer. 'Only don't catch anything until we get there – ha ha!'

Ha ha, indeed! Within five minutes, I had two 3-pound trout on the bank. It was wonderful – or rather it would have been wonderful, had we managed to capture the epic on film. For despite my calls for a camera, not a soul heard, and not a frame was recorded.

When the TV crew did turn up, they were stunned. Someone had the bright idea of retying the trout to the hook and restaging the landing, but I was reluctant and fearful. Anglers are critical viewers and it only takes someone with a slow rewind on a video machine to smell a rat.

As it happened, it did not come to that. For, emboldened by success, I again cast my fly, a tantalising Baby Doll, over the water, and ten minutes later, we had another respectable offering on the bank. Finally, a fishing programme with fish!

We thanked our lucky stars and blessed the river god. But we went away in no doubt about the lessons we had learned from the fish.

Major G.L. Ashley-Dodd

Dry-Fly Fishing for Salmon and Sea Trout

To the best of my knowledge the first serious attempt to fish for salmon with a dry fly originated with the late Major J.R. Fraser CMG in, I think, the year 1906.

The idea of taking it up seriously was suggested to him by the not uncommon occurrence, on the River Test, of a salmon rising at and taking a mayfly when he was fishing for trout on the lower waters which are frequented by salmon.

Being a skilled fly tier, he then tied a series of floating flies more or less on the principle of the mayfly, but of a somewhat stronger construction, and incorporating some of the feathers which from time immemorial have been recognised material for some of the more successful salmon flies. With these he experimented, also entrusting the writer with a duplicate set, in the year 1907.

When fishing for trout on the lower Test we usually carried a stout mayfly cast and one or two of these flies, using them in a precisely similar manner to the ordinary mayfly when we had reason to suspect a salmon in our neighbourhood. At first we had a great measure of disappointment, owing to several causes which I will take in order:

1. We were constantly run out and broken, owing to our only using light trout rods and an ordinary tapered dry-fly line without backing, the salmon often being large and the weeds in the Test being many. The remedy for this, obviously, was a somewhat stiffer rod and plenty of backing, on a rather larger winch: an 11-foot split cane and about 50 yards of backing we found suitable.
2. We often missed a salmon when he rose; this we eventually discovered was by striking too quickly; a salmon, for some reason, closes his lips on a fly in a more leisurely manner than the trout and, therefore, he wants a slower strike. As he generally rises head and tail when taking a floating fly, one usually has plenty of time when fishing up-stream, and my own rule is not to strike till either I see the line tighten or till he disappears on his downward course. The head-and-tail rise is one of the principal attractions of this style of fishing and I think that

every salmon fisherman will agree with me that the mental photograph of individual salmon which have risen to them in this way is indelibly engraved on their memories as one of the greatest thrills which this noble fish can produce.

3. Owing to the wire of the hooks being of necessity very light, we found that the ordinary pattern was very liable to pull out, especially when a weight of weeds was on the line, and so we eventually favoured a double hook with turn-up eye. I know there is a school of fishermen, and good fishermen at that, who dislike the double hook, mainly because they say that one hook tends to lever out the other hook, but this has not been my experience with the small double hooks, especially as the wire of these hooks is thin and has a bit of spring in it. In fact, of late years I have been converted, when using a dry fly for sea trout, into using double hooks on such sizes of trout dry flies as 1 or 0, from the experience I had on the Deveron a few years ago, when a friend presented me with some beautifully tied little flies on double hooks, which he invariably used on that river for brown trout and finnock. He assured me that since he had

used them he had landed a far greater percentage than he had when using single hooks, and begged me to try them. I did so, and certainly as regards fishing for sea trout with a dry fly I am converted. The mouth of the brown trout is so hard that with them it makes little difference, but with the tender mouth of the fresh-run sea trout, I firmly believe that double hooks get a better grip, and I would certainly advise my brother anglers to give them a fair trial. When fishing for brown trout only, I still prefer the single hook, especially when they are highly educated, as no sea trout or salmon can be, owing to his briefer experience of the wiles of man.

Now for a word as to the actual use of the dry fly for salmon: I do not want to infer for one moment that it should be a standard method to be used on all occasions, but I certainly affirm that a dry fly, properly used, will on occasion catch a salmon when any other bait would be absolutely useless.

Take, for instance, a blazing hot day in low water when a salmon can be seen lying under a tree or behind a rock in comparatively shallow water; the ordinary fisherman will look idly at that fish, estimate his weight, and go his way, knowing that in that position and in that light no fly or prawn would move him. Not so the dry-fly man; he will put on his dry fly and fine cast, stalk that salmon just as he would on a chalk stream, and will have a real good chance of getting him when other anglers do not think it worthwhile even to carry a rod.

Under exactly these conditions the writer once killed four salmon in a day (biggest 22 pounds) besides a number of trout, when other fishermen at the same place were telling each other what they would do when a spate came!

There is one radical difference between fishing dry fly for trout and for salmon; if you have any drag on your fly when casting over a trout – down he goes; but very often the converse is the case when a dragged fly comes over a salmon – up he comes!

From my own experience I would recommend that the fly be first put over him a couple of times or so without drag; this will presumably, anyway, not frighten him, even if it does not interest him; then, if he has taken no notice, alter your position somewhat, and get on a drag as artistically as you can about a foot in front of his nose, and keep the fly dragging as long as it will; he will then often turn and take it long after it has passed him.

When fishing a fairly broad river the same rule applies for salmon as for trout, i.e. you need not always be behind him; you may be almost opposite to him, or in cases where you want to operate a drag, you may even be above him, but you must be out of his sight, and you must be sure that he does not catch the flash of your gut; but any man who has fished a southern chalk stream will require no hints as to these matters; they will come naturally to him, and I do not in this chapter pretend to give tips on ordinary dry-fly fishing as practised on such rivers as the Test, Itchen, Kennett, Wylie, etc.

One of the greatest attractions of using the dry fly for salmon is that no matter what the state of the weather or water, except thunder, there is always a chance of killing a fish, which is a great consideration when you have paid a stiff price for an August fishing in Scotland and the water has been too low (often for weeks) to catch a salmon in the normal way, though the salmon are there, getting more listless and sulky every day.

I have also caught many sea trout on an ordinary trout dry fly under similar conditions, especially when I have been favoured with a breeze upstream. Do not forget that when sea trout are, owing to low water, confined in a pool, their nature is not to lie still like salmon (though at times, especially during the middle of the day, they will do so), but they are continually on the wander, so it is neither necessary nor wise for you to move about too much. Keep still, for choice in a spot where there is a background behind you, watch the water, and take occasional casts.

Bob Davison

The Bishop

Monday was his day of complete anonymity; false teeth in pocket, old fishing hat decorated with coloured flies, old trousers, old jacket, old waders and an old, well-used rod. In fact, it looked as he had gone to great lengths to disguise his very well-being. Nobody would even guess that yesterday he had been host to royalty.

He walked at a leisurely pace along the bank until he reached his favourite spot, a finger of heather-clad bank that reached out into the water at the entrance to the bay; a lonely place, shared only with the heron. But it was here that the Bishop found absolute relaxation. In fact, it had become known, unofficially, as 'Bishop's Ripple'.

Placing his rod and tackle against a lichen-covered boulder, he slowly filled his pipe; that, too, was old.

'This is heavy,' he mused.

The sky was overcast, with a steady ripple on the water; perfect conditions, and what's more, the fish were rising to the 'alders'.

'Hmm,' he thought, 'with a bit of luck I might take a trout.' A modest man, an excellent fisherman; none of the big, ugly lures on the bottom, but a dry fly on the surface all the time, and a small one at that!

His previous week had been busy. Several meetings, services, a marriage and of course the highlight of the week, the visit by royalty. So today was going to be a day of relaxation. A friendly goose paddled up alongside as he sat puffing his pipe before commencing casting a fly. Searching his pocket, he found a forgotten biscuit; a bit soft, but it would do. He was continually being scolded by his wife for leaving 'debris', as she put it, in his pockets. 'Quentin,' she would scold, 'really you should burn these smelly old clothes – and the pieces of food I find – really!' He would smile patiently, telling her not to fuss.

He was one of the kindest men I have ever met, In his middle fifties, inclined to be plump, of medium height and with a shock of silver hair which framed his cherub face, the blue eyes shone out from a clear, pink skin: the epitome of a man of God.

I had decided to do a boat patrol during the late afternoon. The lake was well attended, and a word here and there took care of the hour. Soon I reached the spot where the Bishop was fishing but decided not to disturb him, making my way well out into the middle of the lake.

Travelling at low speed so as not to disturb the fish, as I reached abaft of him I raised my hand in salute, and he beckoned me to come alongside. Sitting at the water's edge thoughtfully sucking his pipe, he pointed to a freshly landed rainbow trout of about two pounds.

'Robert, come and look at this – extraordinary!'

I examined the fish. On its side was a mutation – a distinct sign of a cross. It extended down the lateral line of the trout, looking just as if it had been painted. I was astonished; the Bishop, I could see, was deep in thought. 'Truly amazing, Robert,' he murmured gently. I quietly left him and continued my patrol.

During the early evening I was talking to a disappointed angler who had been fishing most of the day without success. He told me that he wanted to catch a little fish for his wife, who was very ill. I sympathised with him, wondering how I could help, when into the office strode the Bishop looking very pleased with himself. He had caught his limit of five rainbows, which he had weighed for his records.

'Hello John, any luck today?' greeted the Bishop.

'No sir, just not my day, I've had a couple on but lost them. Mary will be disappointed,' replied John.

'How is she?' The Bishop knew the family.

'Up and down sir, it's a bit hard, you know.'

From his bag the Bishop reached for a fish. 'Look here, give her this, with my best wishes.'

John was beside himself with thanks. As he left, the man of God reminded me that he was off to Scotland for the next three weeks to fish the lochs. I bade him good fishing.

It was a month later when I next saw John, looking a changed man. 'Good morning John, how's the wife?'

John looked at me with moist eyes. 'It's a miracle, the doctors are puzzled, she is on the mend. Never seen such a change in a person. You know, doctors are wonderful people.'

I left him fishing, he was at peace now.

The Bishop came fishing the next week, and we exchanged news; apparently he had an excellent and fruitful holiday, with a 10-pound salmon to prove it.

'Hope you've stocked the waters since I've been gone Robert.' I reassured him. 'By the way,' he called out as I was about to leave, 'when I last fished, remember that rainbow trout with the mutation?'

'Yes,' I replied.

'Well, when I arrived at the palace I went to show it to my wife, but to my dismay, I found that I must have given it to John. A pity really, the Archbishop was coming on a visit and I would have liked him to have seen it.'

I retraced my footsteps until I was close to him. Looking him straight in the eye, I said, 'My Lord Bishop, may I humbly suggest when you get back to the palace you read Jeremiah 30:17: "For I will restore health unto thee, and I will heal thee of thy wounds, saith the Lord."'

Bob Davison

The General

The General had been a keen and regular visitor to the lakes. As a fisherman I would say he was above average, invariably going home with a brace or two. Inclined to be a loner, and somewhat distant and aloof with his fellow anglers, nevertheless he was a gentleman of the first order. One would find him fishing at least twice a week; that is, apart from his yearly visit to Scotland, when he fished the rivers with his old comrade, the Brigadier.

General R.C. Hodgeman VC – that's the name I shall give him – had seen many years' service in India, during which he had gained the reputation of being an obstinate and most determined man – an empire builder. Although in his late seventies, he still managed to retain his upright, soldier-like bearing. Just a fraction under 6 foot, his face was covered in a mass of tiny red veins – his nose undoubtedly savoured many a 'chota peg' of choice malt. His iron-grey hair was cropped short, with a moustache that could be described as 'tailored by Savile Row'. His strong jaw was deeply set into his once broad shoulders, draped now in Donegal tweed, and his feet were encased in strong brown leather. He would never enter the water: 'Disturbs the fish!' he would growl. The capable hands looked more at home with a service .45 than his Palakona fishing rod.

But despite all this, ever since his encounter with the 'Admiral' he had become a changed man.

The Admiral was the name the fisherman had given to a huge brown trout whose weight had been estimated at about 20 pounds. He had lived for a long time in Clampitt Bay and many rods had fished unsuccessfully for him – he presented the ultimate challenge of the waters. Many times I had seen him take a fly only to spit it out, seemingly with contempt. He resembled a young porpoise as he cruised slowly around his beloved bay; I secretly hoped he was never caught.

The General had become completely obsessed with the big fish and at the crack of dawn, day after day, week after week, he could be seen casting fly after fly, always in the bay, completely disregarding the more easily caught stocked fish. I have never seen such dedication.

As the weeks went by he became very bad tempered; his normally compact tackle could now be seen scattered on the bank, boxes of flies strewn in disorder. With nostrils flared like an impatient filly, he would utter obscenities as he endeavoured to entice the wily old trout. But still the Admiral would cruise just out of range, as though challenging the army to catch him. I am certain that a kind of rapport developed between the crusty old warrior and the brownie.

The August sky took on the appearance of an angry bruise; a freshening wind from the south-west heralded a likely storm. The lake became a mass of tiny wavelets, and it was as if the entire body of water was boiling. The atmosphere seemed charged with an air of foreboding. I knew somehow that something dramatic was about to unfold.

As usual, the General was fishing Clampitt. By now he had become part of the bay, and nobody paid much attention to him, dismissing him as a silly old fool. I had reached the bay after completing half my afternoon patrol, and decided to rest for a while under a granite outcrop that shadowed the little stream trickling into the bay. Lighting a cigarette, I watched the General fish. A terrific splash, accompanied by a high-pitched screech of his line, told me that the brownie had accepted the fly. He'll soon shake that off, I thought, hadn't I seen it all before? However, five minutes gradually gave way to ten: the fish was on!

The General's face was a study; he had become very calm. I could see his jaw muscles flexing as he played the noble fish. The General was again at war. The bay had become the Khyber Pass. The fight lasted a full twenty minutes. I moved in alongside, reluctantly offering to net it for him, but was waved aside with a brusque 'I can manage!'

I retreated to a discreet distance. It had begun to rain, spotting the water as the Admiral was being landed; a couple of inquisitive damselflies hovered above its head, as if bidding farewell. I watched with a feeling of sadness, for I had known this trout for a long time and had even fed it by hand.

And then a most strange thing happened.

The fisherman was about to give the *coup de grâce* when I saw him pause, looking into the trout's eyes. Without a word, he gently removed the fly and slipped the fish back into the water, muttering softly, 'Good luck Admiral, perhaps now I can fish in peace.'

The Admiral is still making a mockery of the anglers – that is, all except one. I have since seen the old soldier feeding the fish by hand. I pretend not to see. He is a different man now; he actually gives me a smile. Needless to say, he never mentions the Admiral. Neither do I.

Chris Dawn

Six Shadowy Shapes

Six shadowy shapes moved across the white coral sand like miniature submarines. They had a sense of purpose. They knew where they were going. Surely they would ignore my gaudy fly?

With heart pounding, and hands trembling, I waited for the signal to cast. Max, the guide, tracked the pod of fish as they moved into the firing line as though they were enemy fighters on a radar screen. 'Twelve o'clock . . . eleven o'clock . . . ten o'clock, now hit 'em.'

One false cast was all that was needed to shoot the number 12 line to intercept the moving fish. But I hesitated for a fatal second before letting fly and the lure landed just behind the main shoal.

'Shit man, who taught you to cast?' Max looked at me pityingly as he spat tobacco juice in the direction of my sandalled foot. 'You just blew the only shot of the morning.'

But had I? A lone silver shape following behind the main shoal turned suddenly and followed my fly. Max woke up suddenly. 'I don't believe it. It's gonna take. Just keep stripping. And if it jumps, remember to point the rod.'

The next few seconds remain a scar in my memory. The great fish engulfed the fly with its cavernous mouth just a few feet from our moored skiff. I could actually see its huge eye looking at me from under the surface.

Yet as soon as it felt the 2/0 hook, the hunted quarry exploded from the water in a frightening display of strength. Some 8 feet of silver-scaled muscle climbed skywards like a Polaris missile. My mouth simply dropped open at such a primitive display of power. And I forgot to point the rod.

That was my first encounter with the tarpon, a fish with the appearance of a giant silver herring and the strength of a saltwater mahseer. And my first lesson in how to play them, or rather how they play you.

Tarpon are a tropical species found worldwide, with a propensity for brackish water in swamps and river mouths. Some of the largest swim in that maze of channels, cays, flats and mangroves that make up the Florida Keys.

That was where I hooked and lost that first 100-pound tarpon all those years ago. And I made a vow then and there to return to Indian Key, off Islamorada, to take my tarpon.

The opportunity was not to present itself until fifteen years later. Back in Islamorada on a bone-fishing trip, my host was amazed to learn that I was still tarpon-less. Despite his assurances that we would catch, the memory of my earlier failure haunted me as we ran at 30 knots along channels no more than a few feet deep. Mangrove branches brushed against my face as top tarpon guide Richard Stanzyck took the short cut out to the main channel where the tarpon had been 'busting'.

The sun was sinking fast in a golden fireball across Florida Bay when we arrived at the channel marker to await the incoming tide. None of the handicap of fly tackle for us tonight. The bait was to be small swimming crabs, hooked in the back and allowed to swim around in the current under a float.

Darkness falls quickly in the tropics, and it was not long before we were engulfed in a velvet blackness, lit only by natural fluorescence from plankton in the water. The navigation lights from other tarpon skiffs blinked across the water. Richard assured me that the tarpon would not be long in arriving.

This style of night fishing is done by feel alone, with the crab held in the tide by the stiff 20-pound glass spinning rod. The first one knows of a tarpon take is a tremendous tug on the rod. This is why the clutch setting on the fixed spool is so important. If it is too tight, the 20-pound mono will simply break like cotton. If it is too loose, the line will pour from the spool without the hook being set.

The first splash of a tarpon feeding in the tide broke my reverie. They crash on the surface like giant rainbows in their hunt for free-swimming crabs. A tension now settled on our boat as we waited. My concentration was starting to wane when three slow clicks of the spool were the overture to a screaming run. 'Point the rod, point the rod,' screamed my guide as he swung his spotlight to a hole in the water which some 60 pounds of tarpon had just vacated.

Too late. Once again I had forgotten the lesson. If one does not point the rod at the fish the moment it jumps, the hook simply rips out of its hard, bony mouth.

Richard was more diplomatic than my previous guide and offered me some solace with a bottle of Miller Draft. I took a few swigs, but the fizzy brew simply stuck in my throat. Tarpon number two had been hooked – and lost. 'Don't worry, We've got another hour before the tide turns,' said Richard as he hooked up another crab for me to lower into the tide and feed away with the current. Shouting and splashing 200 yards away told us that another skiff had successfully hooked up. Next time I would get it right, I told myself – provided there was a next time.

The time ticked away, with Richard looking at his watch. A warm breeze from the south-east gently rocked the boat. An ominous clap of thunder from the distant mainland reminded us that May is the peak season for tropical storms.

Then it happened. The clutch screamed like a banshee while the water exploded with the leaping tarpon. But this time I was ready. And without thinking twice, I pointed the rod at the fish. Now line poured from the reel in ever-increasing amounts. The spool was vanishing fast as Richard pulled up the mooring poles as we went in pursuit of the fish.

'It's big,' said Richard. 'Just keep your cool and keep winding. And don't tighten that drag.'

We set off in the pitch black with the fish towing us in the dark. Was this safe, I asked myself. What if we ran aground? But the fish knew where it was going and ran up the channel, slowed down only by the skiff and two anglers it had to drag behind. I just kept on recovering the 200 yards of line it had ripped from the reel with such ease.

After some forty-five minutes of pure adrenalin rush – it seemed to pass in seconds – the fish started to slow down.

'It's giving up early. You're lucky,' grinned Richard.

'You're in with a chance here.'

I tentatively tightened the clutch to recover more line. So far, so good. Now Richard was able to shine the spotlight on the water to find the giant fish, wallowing in the shallow water. 'Great. It's gone up on a flat. We've got it now.'

For record purposes, the angler has only to touch the short shock, or rubbing, leader, of 100-pound mono. The days of tarpon being dragged back to the boat dock and hung up for the flies to gather belong to the Victorian age, when they were hunted with a similar enthusiasm to tiger and bear.

Richard gingerly eased the great fish to the side of the skiff, where we could admire those scales the size of crowns, and delicately removed the hook with pliers. 'It's gotta go 120 pounds at least. Well done.'

I wished the fish all the best on its tropical journeys as it lay on its side for a moment, before shuddering into life and disappearing into the dark ocean. It had taken fifteen years to achieve my dream of taking a 100-pound tarpon. Now I felt a deep sense of loss.

After such a heart-stopping battle, what else was left in fishing? Yet angling is like a never-ending story, and the lesson I learned in playing and releasing such a formidable fish was to be repeated again and again with lesser, but equally worthy, opponents.

John and Llin Golding MP

The Boat is the Enemy

J**ohn**: 'The boat is the enemy,' wrote Bob Church in one of his excellent books. Bob is truly an expert with a boat. His skill is legendary, using techniques he pioneered himself. One of the most enjoyable mornings of my life was receiving instruction from Bob as we fished Rutland, that inland sea. 'Be tidy!' he begged and for the first time in my life I took notice of this nag. Everything was made easy for me by the way that, slowly and deliberately, Bob put us over the fish. We caught fish steadily and all went well until Bob used the boat as most other experts use it – to row away from the fish!

I used to envy men in boats, but not now. They are there only to entice you away from the bank from which you can fish easily and safely.

The most dramatic example of this was with Cranley Onslow at Bayham during the first Lords and Commons fishing event. (I do not use the word match – we were never a match for anyone.) In the morning I had watched Bob Church and others pulling good trout one after another out of a particular hole which John Parkman had obligingly filled with fish. After a good dinner (lunch to some), I persuaded Cranley to row towards this spot but, although we fished hard in wind and rain, we did not have a touch.

Cranley swore that all the fish were in the middle – or down the other end – or on the opposite side – anywhere but where we were. This, of course, is a common characteristic: the refusal to accept that one is covering fish but leaving them unmoved. 'Let's move,' he said.

'No,' said I. 'Bob Church always leaves one or two.'

Just as the all-party alliance was about to crumble completely, Taff Price staggered down the lawn and, casting against the gale, put his fly under our boat. First cast and he was into a fish. As the hook set, Cranley growled, 'There are no fish here. I'm going further down.'

'Let me see Taff land it,' I pleaded for it was a beauty of 6 or 7 pounds. But Cranley pretended neither to hear me nor to see Taff land his fish. Instead he rowed doggedly away from that fish to a spot which had been declared out of bounds by every fish ever put into Bayham Lake. Of course we caught nothing.

It has been the story of my life ever since. Boatmen are the gypsies of the angling world, happiest when they are on the move.

I did get my own back on Cranley. As we heard thunder I told him how my uncle had been killed by lightening while fishing at my side. I was also hit but survived to tell the tale.

As I said, on that glorious morning at Rutland even Bob Church decided to leave the fish feeding in the waves near the north wall to go after brownies, all fasting like miniature Ghandis in the south. We travelled for miles with Bob slunk in the bottom of the boat as yet another gale blew, looking more miserable on Rutland Water than all his books would have you believe was possible.

I fished constantly at this time with a Rt. Hon. Gentleman whose name I shall not give you; he likes to hide his light under a bushel and so we will call him just the R.H.G. Bob was fishing with the R.H.G., who claimed to have had his hook straightened out by a big brownie on the bottom. I mentioned that I had last seen his fly, when our boats got near, attach itself to our outboard motor, but like Cranley he pretended not to listen. It is an acquired characteristic of successful politicians.

The R.H.G. hates not catching. I remember the day at Bayham when we fished for an hour and a half without touching anything. I explained to him that I was used to going three months without a touch, but he still grumbled about the distance he had travelled that morning for such awful fishing. Then a fish struck and went round and round the boat like a greyhound out of trap 1 at Wimbledon, before tiring and wrapping itself around the anchor chain.

A huge crowd had gathered on the bank to witness this historic event. The fish was firmly fixed to the anchor and the R.H.G. was giddy from having spun round in the boat trying to keep up with it. Normally, I sneak off on such occasions, but all boats are prison ships. Even though I am very clumsy, with poor eyesight, I had to try and net the fish. I pulled up the anchor very slowly, with my heart in my mouth, and slipped the net underneath it. It was with some relief that as I lifted it out of the water I saw that the fish was also in the net.

The crowd cheered. The R.H.G. acknowledged their appreciation of pure skill and for ten minutes or so contemplated the fish in the bottom of the boat before remarking, 'Isn't this a wonderful place!'

It was on this occasion, the very weekend that Maggie had made him a 'Sir' that Geoffrey Johnson Smith, playing a 10-pound plus trout on 2-pound nylon, shouted to us, 'I have no faith in my leader.'

'You ungrateful devil,' I replied. He lost the fish – as ultimately, of course, he lost his leader.

Pete Thompson, a lovely chap even though he is angling correspondent of the *Star*, Radio Stoke, and the *Staffordshire Sentinel*, is another who uses a boat purely for recreational and conservation purposes. He came to the Opening Day at Brookside Fishery, Betley, to see the fun. Under his eagle eye I caught twenty-three good-quality trout in no time. As I watched three more good fish together follow my fly, I heard Pete say: 'If you really want some good sport come to Tittesworth Reservoir with me on opening day.' Of course I went, and of course we blanked. As we got into our boat a young boy of eight or nine years was pulling in his third or fourth fish within 5 yards of the bank. Then we rowed to the middle and caught nothing.

When the R.H.G. rowed away from rising fish in similar circumstances outside the boathouse at Droitwich one bitterly cold winter's day, he explained that the owner had told him where the fish were. We blanked and the owner's brother won the contest fishing from the bank near the boathouse. With Pete Thompson I assumed that, with the zest for truth and accurate detail characteristic of his profession, he had gone out to the middle to get a better view of the bank fishermen and boys catching fish. Anyway, we had an excellent chat, undisturbed by the sordid business of taking fish off the hook.

The club tried to make amends. On my next visit to Tittesworth I was put with a boating expert – an ex-merchant seaman. Unfortunately, he lost his rowlock within ten minutes of the start of an inter-county competition and left me stranded in the muddy mouth of the River Churnett catching one perch after another.

My bad luck with boatmen is legendary. I fished one contest with a Royal Navy officer who, after fifteen minutes, enquired of me which way the wind was blowing. His passion was circumnavigation; his hero Drake rather than Izaak Walton.

But of all the unlucky places where the boat has been the enemy, the worst is Ringstead Grange. I went there for a Bob Church competition. The R.H.G. was to present the prizes and had been practising for a week handing them out with his left hand so that he could receive them with his right.

Alan Pearson showed me where the big trout were and we rowed steadily over them. Unfortunately, the R.H.G. followed Izaak Walton rather than Drake. Every time I spotted a fish he would lose control of the boat and I would hook him instead. He was a bit upset when I did so, but I consoled myself with the thought that he would have been more upset if I had caught a big fish. I would have liked to have stayed with the fish, but the R.H.G. saw boats gathering quickly in the far corner and made for it on the basis that if they were all heading there they must be catching. The probability is that one person was seen to catch a fish and that started a rush.

As we abandoned the fish to Alan Pearson, I thought that all the boats I venture out in should carry the Greenpeace flag to acknowledge that we are on a mission of conservation. Anyway, we caught nowt! The boat really became the enemy in the afternoon, however, when I found myself on the bank watching the R.H.G. trying to unravel his line, which had got into an unholy mess. Having no fish and being desperate for even a pull, I went to cast from the bank while the R.H.G. unravelled to his heart's content. To give me a little greater length (my 4-yard casts seemed inadequate to cover the watery acres) I stood on the end of the boat pulled on to the bank. After a few minutes of intense concentration, which was necessary to get any line out at all, I heard voices behind telling me that now I was in the right spot!

Always ready to receive the cheers of the crowd – the last time had been when I just failed to lose a Labour seat at a by-election in 1969 – I turned around. To my shock and astonishment (I could not swim or row a boat) I was a third or more across the lake. My struggle to cast had rocked the boat off the bank and into the water. My life passed before my eyes but I did not panic. I just prayed that the wind would blow while I carried on casting. It did and I arrived at the other side, where I persuaded an invalid to row me back. I am afraid the R.H.G. was not waiting for me on my return. There was I returning like Nelson from the Nile and he had gone off not only in high dudgeon but also, as he described it later, in a tiny coracle for one. On finishing his unravelling, he had looked up to see me in the middle of the pool and cursed me to all and sundry for 'stealing his boat'.

My only regret is that I was not banned from that fishery for felony for, on my next visit to Ringstead, my experience in one of its boats was even more traumatic. I knew on arrival the day was to be ill-fated – I was paired with Tony Pawson. Now I am accident prone, I have been hit by both bus and lightning – but Tony Pawson makes me look like the man who broke the bank at Monte Carlo. He is truly one of life's natural victims.

I recall the time he came to fish at Mr Barratt's fishery at Betley and in this very well-stocked water caught some excellent fish. In an interview with Pete Thompson for Radio Stoke he put his success down, not to the fact that this is one of the best-stocked fisheries in the country, but to the fact that he used a black fly, for example a Black Pennel.

On hearing this I almost choked. I knew a Black Pennel sat on the wall in Tony's home, a memory of his father who had used it forty years earlier. Tony himself, however, worked on the rule of thumb that one should always use a fly just 4 inches smaller than the fish one is after. Myself, I always worked to 3 inches. Consequently, Alan Pearson had a Pawson Pennel made up; a good 6 inches long on a hook that had last seen service off Hawaii fishing for big marlin.

The bait having been prepared, Tony was then inveigled into taking a group of us one afternoon to a fishing exhibition in Winchester shortly after he had won the World Championship. Before going on to the exhibition we fished that morning at the finest fishery of them all: Avington. While we were casting our lines, my wife Llin was in Winchester placing the huge fly near Tony's even more massive cup with a card informing the world that this was the 'killer fly' used by Tony Pawson on the Test and in the World Championship. We were duly taken from Avington to the exhibition. Of this the only thing I remember is the shock on Tony's face when, from the middle of the room, he spotted that his 'secret' had been laid bare to the world. Llin took a photograph of this moment, which she treasures to this day.

Tony is easily shocked. I recall the occasion when Southern Television were filming the Tony Pawson All Stars and the Lords and Commons Team standing in line after a match. Quietly I suggested to my team mates that they give the thumbs-up sign to the cameras to give the appearance of victory. It took Tony too long to realise that his winning team were to be presented to the world as the good-natured, smiling losers. He learned the hard way that even if we could not catch fish, we could catch him!

He still remembers it to this day. He remembered it recently when we filmed together at Avington. Well, that is not quite right; the TV people said they wanted two people, one an extrovert to face the camera and one who could be relied upon to catch a fish in order to hand it over immediately to the presenter to land as if he had caught it. Naturally they insisted on Tony for the camera job.

There are many other incidents I could dwell on, such as when he caught me changing the pegs in the moonlight before a Lords and Commons match in a vain attempt to give that team a chance of not coming bottom yet again. But I have said enough for you to understand why I knew that the day at Ringstead was going to be a disaster.

We went in a boat, but the weather was so bad that we used it only to cross the pool. It was a foul day. Once again we had to face a gale and blinding rain. Tony caught a fish and I had my usual blank. After hours of flogging the water, we heard the R.H.G. hoot as he passed by on his way to dinner. We decided to take the boat back and join him in the pub to find out how he had done. I particularly wanted to do this because I knew he would restore my confidence by assuring me that the proprietor had been much too busy during the previous week to stock.

I do not row. It is one of those things, like home decorating, that I decided early in my life was beyond me. After I had stumbled into the boat, dragging my gout and arthritis with me, Tony pulled away. Very shortly I noticed the boat was filling up with water. Being conscious of the responsibilities of a cox (although I went to a greensite university, I did listen to the boat race on the wireless), I shouted a warning to Tony. He took not a blind bit of notice. I shouted again. He rowed like a bat out of hell as the veritable Toad would have done. I sat like Mole, frightened and ignored. Suddenly, the blindingly obvious struck him. 'We are sinking!' he shouted. 'We are going down.'

The rest of this story is a matter of controversy. Tony tells a different version, but who would trust a man who once spread the dubious story that our editor, while giving a casting lesson, caught the fly in his own ear? Would I, after seventeen years as a politician, embroider a story or be economical with the truth?

Once in the water, I upturned the boat to grab hold of it as I had been taught to do in a thousand disaster movies. Thank God there are no sharks, I thought, confident that they could not live in water barren of smaller fish to eat. Above the noise of the wind and the rain I heard an anguished cry: 'You shouldn't have done that – now I've lost my fish.' This was an extraordinary fish which he claimed at the time was a 7-pounder but which, in print later, became 8 pounds. Goodness knows what size it is today, certainly a world record breaker. Despite this, because I could not swim he began to pull me to the shore. I was quite content because I was wearing a lifejacket and the proceedings seemed eminently more pleasant and convivial than a meeting of Labour's National Executive with Tony Benn.

All was going well until I heard anxious voices shouting, 'Turn him over!' This puzzled me because I was perfectly satisfied with my position. However, they made me aware that Tony, who had been pulling me, had blacked out and his face was going under.

As these were the days in the Labour Party when the going was hard and I was used to people leaving me to bear the brunt I just shrugged my shoulders and adjusted to the situation. I put Tony right way up and pulled him to the shore where Bob Morray, another superb boatman who taught me much, did a marvellous job literally bringing Tony back from the dead. Although I had got him to the shore they treated me as though I had foulhooked him, and left me to recover on my own.

The ambulance came and Tony and I were taken to the local hospital. He recovered in the ambulance and began to talk a lot of gibberish but, as he had always been on the employers' side in industrial relations, I took that for granted. In the hospital we were visited by a local police sergeant who came to ask what had happened. Tony gave his account but as he had blacked out it was somewhat imaginative. I, of course, having been conscious all the time and used to continual crisis, which was the norm those days in the Labour Party, coolly gave the truth. Faced with these contradictions, the sergeant looked flummoxed. Suddenly he slapped shut his notebook, put his pencil in his top pocket and declared, 'This is a job for the Chief Constable.'

Tony did not immediately have a good time. Phoning Ringstead for his non-fishing clothes he was told to get off the line because there was a crisis in the fishery – the cow was having a calf! Subsequently he was banned for life from the fishery after writing a prize-winning letter to an angling journal on the subject of the inadequacy of the boats.

Worse was to come! He, Tony Pawson, who had played football and cricket for England and was then world fly-fishing champion, read in the *Daily Telegraph*, 'Yesterday, Mr John Golding, the Labour MP for Newcastle-under-Lyme, was saved from drowning by an unknown angler.'

He was distressed by the 'unknown angler' bit and has never recovered, but I was shocked to read that the man I had pulled out, thanks to my lifejacket, was reported to have saved me. The whole incident was turning into a nightmare. I had lost all my tackle – rods, reels, maggots, the lot – when the boat turned over. Then no one turned up that evening to hear me speak at a union meeting because the TV report had put me at death's door and the members assumed I would not be with them. Later, at a time when I was working literally eighteen hours a day, a woman wrote complaining that I was fishing on a Monday and asking why I did not work nine to five like everyone else.

But how did the *Daily Telegraph* get the story so wrong and how did Tony, on the strength of this report, subsequently get a Royal Humane

Society award, along with Bob Morray? It was not as I first thought that he had been granted it for throwing me back, an act of humanity to mankind. Rather that it lay in the fertile imagination of the present Member of Parliament for Newcastle-under-Lyme, Llin Golding. On being inundated with press enquiries about the incident she, being very fond of Tony, made up a wonderful story about his heroism in saving me from the deep! Truth to tell, she was a little surprised herself when she quizzed Bob Morray (who had certainly saved Tony) a few months later about those events. 'Bob,' she asked, 'when you saw Tony go under and you knew John couldn't swim, why didn't you go in to save them?'

'Well, Llin,' said Bob, 'I was thinking of doing so but I remembered I had some new Damart on and I was thinking I would have to take that off first!'

The boat *and* the boatmen are the enemy!

You would think that after this I would never go out in a boat again. Well, of course I did. I am an idiot. But I will hand over to Llin to continue the story as it appears in the House of Commons *Hansard* for 1 March 1995 *Activity Centres (Young Persons' Safety) Bill:*

Mrs Llin Golding (Newcastle-under-Lyme): I shall tell a brief story which illustrates that even Members of Parliament sometimes behave stupidly. (Hon. Members 'Surely not.') Even on St David's Day, I have to say that two Welsh Members of Parliament behaved stupidly – myself and my hon. Friend the Member for Cynon Valley (Mrs Clwyd), whom I visited when on holiday in Wales. She has a boat at Aberdovey.

We decided to go fishing in the bay. My hon. Friend has a small sailing boat that she uses to reach a yacht that she keeps in the harbour. She had never been out in the bay and uses the boat only for access, so it was kept to a standard that was not fitted for going out in the bay. We did not consider that.

We donned our life jackets and decided that we were safe. It was a beautiful day. There was not a breath of wind, the sea was flat calm and it was beautifully warm – tee-shirt-and-shorts weather. We took our rods and went out into the bay using a motor on the small sailing boat.

We fished for an hour with boats all round us, then we turned to come back in. We had almost reached the harbour entrance when the motor cut out. We had run out of petrol. We thought that we could just manage to row into the harbour entrance, even though the tide was going out. We looked for oars, but there was only one. The little holes to put them through were missing as well. (Hon. Members: 'Rowlocks.') That shows how much I know about these things.

We started to go round in circles as we paddled and I decided to hoist the sail. There is a little thing on the end to fasten it. That was missing. We tried to hold the sail, but there was no wind. We started to drift out to sea. We drifted and drifted. At the harbour entrance there are two big sand banks, which are dangerous. We drifted and became worried because the tide had not turned. By now, no one was in sight.

We looked for a flare. There was none. We kept paddling but drifted on to a sand bank. We were in about 18 inches of water, so my hon. Friend the Member for Cynon valley and I jumped out, heroes in the making.

While my husband sat holding the thing that is used to point the boat in the right direction—

Ms Glenda Jackson (Hampstead and Highgate): Rudder.

Mrs Golding: No, something else. We jumped out and pushed the boat, running along the sand bank laughing. My hon. Friend said, 'Don't let go of the boat, because we could suddenly drop into very deep water.'

As the words came out of her mouth, we dropped into very deep water. The boat started to fill with water, because all the weight – the engine, my husband, my hon, Friend and myself – was on one side.

The boat swung around and waves started coming off the sand bank, filling the boat even quicker. The drag was pulling us both underneath. If we had not been wearing life jackets we would have been in a much more serious position.

My husband grabbed us on either side. He swears to this day that he was working out who had the biggest majority. However, he pulled in my hon. Friend the member for Cynon Valley, which of course filled the boat even further, and, with enormous difficulty – the drag was very strong – they managed to pull me in.

I looked for the thing to scoop the water out.

Ms Glenda Jackson: The bailer.

Mrs Golding: That is the word. I whipped my hon. Friend's hat off and started bailing with it. The other two struggled to turn the boat round to prevent the water from coming in and filling the boat as fast as I was trying to empty it.

We eventually drifted on to the shore, where my husband was sent off to get petrol – it being a man's job to get petrol – from a petrol station across the sand dunes, about 4 miles away. Fortunately, he got a lift. When he returned, we filled up the tank and sorted everything out. By then, we were extremely cold. Then we had to return into the bay to go round to get into the harbour. I heard later that the sand bank was full of that stuff – I cannot think of its name –

Mr Merchant: Sharks.

Mrs Golding: No, the stuff that sucks people down. (Hon. Members: 'Quicksand.') Yes. It really was frightening. When we eventually returned, we found that my hon. Friend's husband had been sitting on the balcony, watching our exploits. We had been out for six hours rather than two, and when we asked him if he had been worried about us, he said, 'Not at all. It's a lovely day, the sea is flat calm, and I could see the boat. No problem.'

John: You see what lengths Llin will go to just to catch one tiny mackerel even though, for her also, the boat is the enemy. Of course, when Bob Church wrote that the boat is the enemy he was talking from the point of view of the fish.

Some people claim that fish are stupid but fish do stay away from boats, they do search for food near to banks, and they do learn to swim at an early age without blacking out, or indeed running out of petrol. We can all learn a lot from fish.

Francis T. Grant

Instinct

Fishing for salmon can be thought of as a way of escaping to more primitive times, when man was a hunter in pursuit of his quarry. The most successful hunter is the man who has the greatest understanding of his prey and its habits. This understanding can develop to such a level that it becomes what I call instinct. This is when the hunter suddenly becomes uncannily aware of the location of his quarry, and what it is going to do next, without having any visible or tangible evidence on which to base his knowledge. The phenomenon is not unique to angling, but manifests itself in different ways throughout our daily lives. Generations of modern city living, or the stresses and strains of working life, may mask the symptoms, but I think that many people still have this intuitive ability. How often does one hear or read that 'I felt that I was being watched'? If the person being watched did not know of, or hear the watcher, how was the presence felt? The next time that you find someone reading your newspaper over your shoulder on the underground, think about how you knew of their scrutiny.

In other field sports, such as stalking, or walking up grouse and partridge, many people have suddenly found themselves aware of the presence of game before it showed itself. Even in non-field sports as diverse as mountaineering, motor racing and ocean sailing, there have been many accounts of people's feelings of impending triumph or disaster. Anglers are certainly not unique in reporting such instances of prescience. I know that many people would ascribe these accounts to the angler's experience and knowledge, saying that he was subconsciously aware of some subtle shift in river conditions that made it more likely that a salmon would take. Sometimes this is certainly true, but on other occasions I have been unable to find any explanation for that tense nervous feeling that something is going to happen *now*, or that sudden urgency to be fishing in a different pool, or to put down the sunk line and pick up the floating line, or vice versa.

If, on an otherwise fishless day, when I have not seen a sign of a salmon for several hours, or even all day, and I am not approaching any lie of particular note with my fly, and there has been no change in water height, temperature, or colour, nor any alteration in air temperature, wind strength and direction, amount of ambient light, nor any other environmental factor that I could think of, how is it that I am suddenly aware of that 'butterflies in the stomach' feeling, and of concentration at peak level, to be followed a few seconds later by the take of a salmon, the only fish of the day?

Certainly, it is natural for me to become tense with anticipation when my fly begins to cover the waters of a lie that I know to be highly productive, particularly if accompanied by a positive environmental change, such as a period of warm sunshine on an otherwise bitterly cold grey day in March. However, it is not the same feeling as the one that I believe to be purely instinct. Over the years I have grown to trust these peculiar hunches. The more relaxed I am, and the more that I feel 'tuned in' to the river and the salmon, the more likely I am to experience this odd prescience. If I am worried about something unrelated, and not concentrating as hard as I should be on the fishing, then it is less likely to happen.

As I usually fish by myself, it is rare for me to have a witness on the bank to whom I can say 'I think I am going to get a fish in a few seconds' time . . . Here he is!' although it has happened. I cannot forget one particular incident when there were witnesses to my extraordinary confidence before the event. It happened on 28 April 1982, and I look back on the incident as being one of the milestones of my salmon-fishing career.

It was a cold, cloudy day with a very strong, chill northerly wind blowing. There was little evidence of fish in the beat, although the river was at quite a nice height of about 1 foot 10 inches. Forcing a line out into or across the wind had been exhausting, and by six o'clock in the evening I was cold, weary, fishless, and dispirited. The rest of the party had fared and felt the same. The wind had been so strong that one unfortunate member had been blown off his feet by a contrary gust while wading down in the Bulwarks. Everyone was so tired from the effort needed to fish in a near gale-force wind all day, that we decided not to go out in the evening after supper as usual, but to enjoy a full and leisurely dinner at the hotel instead.

Half-way through the meal, I was suddenly smitten by the thought that I ought to be fishing the Inchbares. Outside the hotel window, conditions had, if anything, deteriorated. The wind was now definitely gale force, with the trees lashing to and fro, and fallen branches being blown along the ground. The urge to go and fish the Inchbares was so strong that I could not resist its compulsion. Pudding was being served when I announced that I had decided to go out again. The rest of the party were more than mildly astonished by my abrupt change of mind. However, enthusiasm and excitement were radiating from me to such an extent that I persuaded two of the others to go out as well. Hurriedly I finished my pudding, declined the previously intended, and seductive temptation of coffee and a leisurely drink after the meal, and left to don waders and coat.

I was standing outside the hotel, doing up my jacket, when Rachel

Henley came out. The conviction that I should not only be fishing the Inchbares, but that I would be successful as well, was so powerful that I was already smiling in anticipation. Rachel took one look at this wolfish grin all over my face. 'You're going to get a fish, aren't you?' It was a statement, not a question.

'Yes, I know,' I nodded, still grinning. My friends know that I am not usually rash enough to make such an incautious statement, but this was no ordinary occasion. I knew without doubt that I was going to catch a salmon.

Parking my car, I walked down across the bare field towards the stile. The gale was blasting the fine topsoil from the field in a reddish cloud, but I ignored the grit getting into my eyes and mouth as I hurried down. Normally, after finishing at around six o'clock, I tie on the flies that I will be using when I start fishing again in the evening after supper. On this occasion, because I had had no intention of going out in the evening, I had not changed them, and I would now have to swap my two half-inch tubes for a couple of threequarter-inch ones. Gripped by urgency and excitement, I opened my fly box a little incautiously, with the result that the wind immediately removed most of the contents. I then had to spend a few minutes furiously scrabbling around in the grass, trying to recover what I could, but at last I was ready to begin.

The wind was howling downstream and a little onshore. I could get my line out across it, but it was a waste of time trying to mend it or otherwise slow the passage of my fly through the water.

I was no more than a third of the way down the Upper Inchbare when I had my first contact. There was a swift double pull on the line, and the reel sounded briefly. I raised the rod, tightening into the fish. He gave a couple of thumps, and the hook came out. Impatiently I checked my flies. Everything was in order.

I resumed casting, optimism and urgency undiminished. Within a couple of minutes I was into another salmon. This was a nice fish of about 12 pounds, but after two or three minutes, the fly again pulled out.

This was disappointing, but I was still gripped with impatience, and the certainty of success. I fished down the pool till I was only 20 yards above the bottom of the Upper Inchbare, and my flies were covering the top of the Lower Inchbare. Behind one of the rocks at the junction of the two pools I hooked another fish. After I had tightened into it, this fish swam straight upstream, right through the pool, till it reached a point level with the groyne at the top. I moved back a few yards inshore till I was standing under the bank. The salmon then turned round, and swam back downstream along the border between the calm water behind the groyne and the turbulence of the current. As it came towards me I reeled in and hurriedly unshipped my net. Obligingly the fish continued to swim down the discontinuity between fast and slack water towards me. When it reached a point about 4 or 5 yards upstream, I took two quick paces away from the bank, stuck my net out, pulled the rod hard over inshore, and the fish swam straight into the mouth of my waiting net. Only when I lifted it from the water did it realise its plight, and how foully I had tricked it. Safe in my net, all its furious lashing was to no avail. It had taken less than two minutes from the time it was hooked till it was in the landing net.

Having resumed fishing, I did not have to wait long – perhaps a quarter of an hour – before I hooked another salmon. However, after four or five minutes' straightforward play, and for no good reason that I could think of at the time, again the hook pulled out.

After rechecking my flies, I carried on, wading down perhaps a rod's length out from the bank, casting into the storm-tossed near darkness. Approaching the bottom, as I made a cast I had an impression that something did not sound quite as it should, although it was very difficult to tell because of the wind. Suspecting that there might be a slight tangle of flies and leader, foolishly I decided to let it fish round before examining it. A few seconds later, there came a hard pull from midstream, followed within a fraction of a second by another, and then the reel screamed, rising into a shrieking protest as something big turned, and hurtled down river at high speed.

By the time I covered the 3 or 4 yards to the bank, the fish was already about 120 yards below me, and although I flung myself up the steep bank, and out of the river, it had travelled at least 150 yards downstream before I could set off in pursuit.

'Probably foul-hooked,' I thought, 'but how could that have happened?' I wondered, as I started to run as fast as I could in chest waders after it. My reel was still shrieking as it emptied at speed, and I was now becoming worried about how little backing I had left, and also about whether the reel would overheat. Fortunately, after I had covered about 40 yards down the bank in pursuit, it began to slow, and stopped taking line off the reel. I continued to run after it, reeling in as I went, and brought it to a halt after I had covered perhaps 60 or

70 yards. At this point the fish was a good 250 yards below where it had been hooked. I carried on walking down the bank towards it, reeling in as I went.

After a short time, it turned and started to head back upstream. Gratefully, I made my way back along the bank, continuing to reel in as the fish followed. I had recovered all but about 70 yards of line and backing, and moved about 50 yards upstream from the lowest point I had reached, when the fish leaped, turned, and set off downstream at high speed again. I followed, and managed to bring it to a halt after it had covered about 80 yards.

Reeling in, I closed the distance till the fish was about 50 yards away, out in the middle of the river and downstream. It leaped clear of the water, crashing back in and then, again. It was much too dark now for me to see, but it sounded like a big fish, probably over 20 pounds. It moved upstream for about 20 yards, and jumped again with a splash, clearly audible over the wind. It then headed diagonally upstream away from me, and without warning the fly came out.

I examined my leader. My suspicions were correct on both counts. Over one of the tail fly's treble hooks was a small white scale, obviously from the belly of the fish. Also, the nylon leader was looped round the back and caught between the shanks of the hooks. It had been pinched so thin that it was remarkable that it did not break during the fight. What seemed to have happened was that due to the wind, or my bad casting, the tail fly and its treble became separated and the nylon slightly tangled, as I had feared. When the fish took, there were probably several inches, if not a foot, between the tail fly and the entangled treble. With the fly in its mouth as it turned away, the trailing treble was drawn up and hooked it, possibly in the region of the pectoral fins, despite the hook points being at right angles to their normal orientation. No wonder it had bolted downstream so spectacularly.

Resolving that never again would I allow any suspicion of a tangle to pass uninvestigated, I headed back for home. Although I had landed only one fish out of the five hooked, I had enjoyed a most exciting evening filled with drama. However, the dominant thought that recurred frequently during the succeeding weeks and months was why had I chosen to go out at all, and why had I been so certain of encountering salmon? I could find no logical explanation.

Everyone in the party had made an active and joint decision not to go out, but to enjoy a leisurely dinner together instead. During the meal, conditions outside were even worse than during the day. The others had made no report of large numbers of fresh fish entering the bottom of the beat, or any other encouraging sign. Why then had I been smitten with this urge to fish the Inchbares, but not any of the other pools on the beat? This burning desire, and sudden enthusiasm had been so strong that not only had I decided to break up the happy party and go out myself, but I had also persuaded others to go out as well. My absolute certainty had been so unmistakable that it had been recognized, and commented on, by others. 'You're going to get a fish,' said Rachel Henley. 'Yes, I know,' was my reply.

My only explanation for the event remains that of hunting instinct, part of the unseen hand that sometimes guides our footsteps. The more I thought about the incident, the more I realised that there existed intriguing angles to salmon fishing which I had not previously guessed at. This rekindled my enthusiasm for the sport, and my approach to it became far more serious, and thoughtful. In turn, this increased my intellectual satisfaction and enjoyment, because instead of fishing mechanically, I was trying to work out why things happened, what the problems were, and how to solve them.

I have come to trust my hunches, particularly about the method that I should use, or which pool I should fish. Perhaps obeying these hunches boosts my confidence and concentration, and that may help the way I fish my fly. I cannot prove that I would not have been successful if I had not followed my instincts. However, I have satisfied myself that it is wise to pay attention to my subconscious. Others may pooh-pooh this as all a figment of my imagination, or coincidence, or a product of my judgement based on the knowledge and experience acquired over many years of salmon fishing. I know what I believe, and that is what is important to me.

Two other examples, the first of instinct telling me 'where', and the second telling me 'how'. Neither occurred in front of witnesses, but both show why I believe so strongly that I am likely to be rewarded if I follow my instinct.

The first took place on 2 May 1984. The river was at 2 feet 9 inches in the morning, falling to 2 feet 5 inches by late afternoon. Apart from a few clouds very early on there was brilliant sunshine all day. I started off in the Slips, and caught first a 7-pounder, and then a beautiful fish of 17 pounds. Ordinarily, I would have gone down the pool again, having already caught two salmon, to see if there were any more, but I had a growing impatient urge to be fishing the Flats. I could not ignore it. So I moved down and in the Lower Flat I struck gold, or rather silver. In rapid succession I hooked five fish and landed three, at 14, 9 and 8 pounds respectively. The two losses were both avoidable errors. One occurred while I was walking the fish up to the intended landing place, when I put my foot carelessly into a hole in the bank. Trying to maintain my balance, my rod tip had dropped, the fish (in the middle teens) had given a hard pull on a direct line, and the dropper knot gave way. The second had shed the hook while I had been concentrating on freeing my net from its entanglement with an ash branch on the bank, and momentarily allowed the fish a slack line. While all this action was taking place, I had been trying to eat my picnic lunch by snatching a couple of bites from a sandwich and a mouthful of beer after each fish was landed or lost, and before dashing back into the river for the next. The protracted meal took till mid-afternoon to consume. After the last fish I had a sudden feeling that there were no more in the pool for me, and that I ought to move on down below the bridge, specifically to the Floating Bank. Normally I would go back up to try the Slips again, but instinct had already proved itself to be spectacularly right once that day, so who was I to doubt it? I moved down, changing from an intermediate to a floating line to cope with the slower waters of the Floating Bank. Sure enough, I caught another beauty, which took the total for the day to seven fish weighing over 80 pounds, an average of 11½ pounds per fish. In memory it remains a day's flyfishing of near perfection. I have never thought that I would have caught so many salmon if I had not trusted my instinct and moved down when I did, and to where it told me to go.

The other incident I have chosen was not so spectacular, and rather more typical of my everyday fishing. It happened on 29 April 1988. After a few bright intervals early on, the day became dark and overcast, with a chilly wind blowing from the north. The water temperature was steady at around 43°F, as was the level at 1 foot 9 inches on the gauge. I started off with the big sunk fly in the Top Gannet, and quickly caught a slightly pink fish of just under 12 pounds at the top of the pool. I covered the rest of the pool without further offers, and moved down to fish the Middle Gannet. There was no response, so I returned to the Top Gannet, and fished it down again with the sunk fly. However, while fishing it, I was ill at ease and conscious that I was doing something not quite right, but I could not identify my fault. A third of the way down the pool, at the corner of the gravel shelf, I hooked a salmon, but I was not surprised when this shed the hooks after two or three minutes' play.

Returning to the water with my sunk fly, I was still disturbed by the belief that I was doing something wrong. After a little while my doubts began to resolve themselves, and I became conscious of a growing conviction that I ought to be fishing the floating line. Soon I found myself hurrying to finish the pool, which I did without further incident. I checked the water temperature, which was unchanged at 43°F. It was still heavily overcast, and the north wind was as cold as ever. There was no perceptible improvement in conditions. Yet, with my floating line and two half-inch Hairy Mary tubes, I waded in again at the top of the pool, confident that I was doing the right thing. Sure enough, with the fly on the dangle less than half-way down the pool, I had a firm take. This turned out to be a beautifully fresh sea-liced salmon of just over 10 pounds. After landing it, I returned to the river, but my confidence in the floating line began to evaporate as swiftly as it had appeared. By the time I finished the pool, I had become convinced that the floating line would not produce another fish for me that day. In the event I was right, and my only other fish fell to the sunk fly. I cannot prove that the 10-pounder would not have taken the sunk fly, but I do know that I made a change in my tactics in response to my instinct, and I caught the fish.

So if I have any advice of the subject, it is to have faith in these subconscious judgements or instinct, however you choose to think of them. I do know that the more that I am tuned in to the river, the more likely that I am to be aware of, and to respond positively, to these hunches and that as a result I will fish better, and be more successful. It can mean the difference between catching nothing and catching several fish a day. Confidence can play a big part in making sure that I am more relaxed, and that my subconscious is not clouded by worry or self-doubt.

This communication that seems to pass somehow between fish and angler is, I think, a part of the curious relationship between prey and predator, the hunted and the hunter. It is a paradox that we anglers who enjoy killing salmon also care more deeply about them than the rest of society. After all, it is the voices of anglers that are the first to be raised in protest at the impact of excessive netting or pollution.

I know that I have a deep emotional involvement with salmon. Having been in the water in a wet suit with them, their effortless, dazzling speed and manoeuvrability is part of the attraction, but I cannot find words to explain it all.

Perhaps part of the attraction of salmon fishing lies in this curious love-hate relationship, that one can love salmon deeply and still enjoy killing them. It may also provide a partial explanation for the phenomenon of the salmon angler's hunting instinct. The most successful anglers may well be those who care most deeply about their salmon, and therefore understand them best, and are most likely to be sensitive to their moods even if they have no conscious realisation of this, and so are able to detect this subconscious identification of prey to predator, and make use of it.

Hunting instinct is an important part of, and perhaps a manifestation of, the bond that ties the hunter to the hunted. For me it is an indication of the depth of my attachment to the sport, and to my quarry. Salmon fishing provides an escape from the bureaucracy, incompetence, self-ishness, dishonesty and unreliability that make much of modern society so tiresome. It provides a rare challenge, both physical and mental, of glorious unpredictability.

If the hunter loves the quarry he pursues, he will not kill in greater numbers than permitted by the natural regeneration of the stock. Nor will he carry on taking fish, regardless of how many are present, if their capture ceases to be a challenge. On several occasions (the first was as long ago as 1970), I have stopped fishing for the day, although at the time I knew I could have carried on catching fish without effort. When salmon fishing ceases to be a challenge, the fun goes out of it. The true sportsman knows this, and also that a deep love and understanding of his quarry is essential to the real enjoyment of his sport.

Edward R. Hewitt

Fishing for Salmon

About an hour or so after sunset, when it is just getting dark, salmon which have been settled in a pool nearly all begin a cruise of the pool, generally first going to the lower end, supposedly to look and see if the water is right for them to continue their progress upstream. If an angler locates himself just above where the water begins to run out of the lower end of a pool and can arrange to fish the water where it is from 18 inches to 2 feet deep and picks out the right place from the look of the bottom and the water flow, and casts continually over such water when he knows there were no salmon there when he took up his position, he will very often be rewarded by hooking fish which is cruising to the lower end of the pool in this shallow water. When the water is rather low and clear in a salmon river, I believe that most of the fish in a pool make this cruise to the lower end as soon as it gets dark enough. I remember one pool on the Patapedia which held six salmon which we had not been able to interest in any of our flies during the daytime. I told my companion, Mr Goodrich, to locate himself on a white stone I had picked out and to fish across the river in the shallow water and to continue until he hooked a fish. He began just before it was dark enough and cast perhaps ten minutes and then said he was going to the head of the pool to try. I urged him to stay where he was, as I was sure he would get a fish. However, he went up the pool and I took his place on the white rock. I had only cast about five minutes when I was fast on to a good fish which I had a lot of trouble in landing because it wanted to go out of the pool, but I finally got it ashore on the beach without a gaff. Then I resumed my place on the rock and in a few casts hooked another which I also managed to land. By that time it was late and I made my way to our tent, with two good fish which I could not get in the daytime at all.

On another trip in Newfoundland we were coming down Harry's Brook with not much luck and camped at dark on a good pool. We thought it was too late to fish so we went to bed. It was so dark when we camped that we picked a place for the tent where the ground had been burned over. About midnight the punkies came out of that burned ground and almost ate me alive. I could not sleep, so I got up and put on my waders and went out in the pool, as the moon had come up and I could see fairly well. Of course, I did not know the pool as I had never fished it, but I cast where I thought the fish might be. I had not been fishing more than a few minutes when I was fast to a large fish which I played, and yelled for help to get it in, waking up the camp. After that I got another good 20-pound fish out of the same pool. During the day we took nothing at all.

On the Gander River, on one of my trips, we were camped alongside a very large and rather shallow pool where I had seen many salmon which I could not raise in the daytime. About eleven o'clock the moon came up opposite our camp and shone across the water. Towards the tail of the pool I could see many lines moving in the water and asked the Indian guide what they were. He said these lines were made by the back fins of salmon cruising the pool. I asked if they would take and he said they would not, but I got on my waders and went out where I could cast the fly so that it would swing over the shallow water at the outlet of the pool where I saw the lines made in the water. I used a very small wet fly and a long leader.

I only made two casts before I had a good fish which I played and brought ashore to gaff. I waded out again and immediately took another fish, and this went on until I had taken seven, which was all I cared for in one night, as it was getting very late. In the daytime it was most difficult to get any fish from this pool, and another party which was camped there had been unable to get one for food in three days. It looked to me as if these fish were sleeping in the daytime and awake at night. This was on 16 August and these fish had not long been in this pool.

These experiences show that there are times when salmon can be caught on a fly far better at night than in the daytime.

Any observant fisherman will have noticed that salmon break water in a number of different ways. No doubt most men let it go at that and do not realise that the kind of break may mean a great deal to their success in fishing. Careful watching may save much time and lead to the capture of many salmon which might otherwise be in little danger of being taken.

For myself, I have long since divided these breaks into different classes and each has its separate meaning. The most frequent rise of the salmon at the surface is the ring it makes in the water, similar to a trout or bass, but generally larger and more marked than either. This occurs when the salmon is taking something at the surface, or very near the surface, into its mouth. The ring is made sometimes by its mouth, which makes a suction close to the surface, to take in the fly, or by its tail as it turns away, having taken the insect just below the surface. In either case the fish is feeding and the angler certainly ought to make it come to a fly if he is skilful and uses the right tackle. If the fish is taking a fly off the surface, a dry fly surely ought to raise it. If it is taking larvae below the surface, a small wet fly in the nymph style of fishing will probably prove far better. In either case, such a fish should be made to come to a fly if it is properly selected and cast. These fish are also often taken on a wet fly in the regular way.

Next, you may notice a salmon rolling; that is, coming to the surface and showing its head and generally its back fin. Such a fish is generally taking the larvae of flies just below the surface; it is a feeding fish. It is very rare when such a fish cannot be caught with a nymph fly or small wet fly.

Sometimes the salmon breaks water with a great splash like a trout. This is when it has made a rapid rush for the fly from some distance away and is unable to stop when it gets to the surface. It also is a feeding fish, and ought to be easily caught.

When, however, you see a salmon leap from the water, its whole body thrown into the air, with its head up and gill plates and mouth closed tight and its throat drawn in, and fall upon the surface of the water on its side or belly with a great slap, you need not waste any time fishing for it because you will never get that fish at that time. It is in pain from the growth of the melt or roe sacs inside its body and is jarring itself to settle the sac or break down some small adhesion formed in the body cavity. In all my experience I have never caught a fish I saw jump in this way. You may get another fish in the same locality but not this one. This form of leap is much more frequent in the late season, when the sacs get larger and occupy more space in the body.

I always watch all breaks with the greatest care, as they not only show the location of the fish, but often indicate just how to fish for them in the surest way.

CONCLUSION

Although now over eighty-one, I am still able to fish streams and find it most pleasant to have tea at five o'clock at my house on the hill and then drive down to the Neversink and fish until dark. There are always plenty of trout, but it is not every evening they will rise well. It is these hard fishing times which I enjoy most. I try to find out how to take these difficult trout and almost always return them to the water when I have done so. I am certain I caught one individual trout, which I called 'Tubby' seventeen times last year without injuring him at all. It is delightful to have my old friends visit me and to watch them have a good time fishing. It is wonderful to watch the evening light come on and the night finally take the place of day. This is what is happening to me; the evening is coming on pleasantly, and the night will soon take its place according to the order of nature.

While I have no doubt killed more fish than I should at times . . . I hope I have made some amends by what I have been able to do for my friends the fish, and also for my friends the fishermen.

May we meet along the stream, and if not there, then in the happy fishing grounds of the Micmac Indians in the hereafter. I only hope it may aid you, if only in some small way, to have as much pleasure as I have had on the rivers. On parting with one of our guides, as we left home, he remarked: 'When you die, Charon will have to stop the boat on the Styx and let you fish; he could never get you across the river.' I only hope I may have one last chance to see if I can raise one there also.

And now with Walton, 'Blessings upon all that hate contentions, and love quietness, and virtue, and Angling.'

John Waller Hills

A Good Mayfly Day

It was one of those days which May sometimes brings. The sun shone, the sky was blue and silver, the breeze was light and the trees were all a different shade of green. The water meadows were bright with flowers. The liquid gold of the kingcup was fading, but there were wide drifts of the delicate lilac of the cuckoo flower, whilst in the dryer spots rich yellow cowslips were mixed with dark purple orchids. The broad Test ran full and fast and stainless. I started at ten o'clock in the morning, knowing that at some time during the day the mayfly would appear.

For a time nothing happened. I strolled to the bottom of my beat, to have it all ahead of me. At last the first mayfly sailed down, followed by another and another. Still no trout rose. But at length there was a movement, though the fish was certainly under water. I put on a hackle fly, wetted it and cast 2 feet above him. The fly fell softly on the smooth surface, and gently disappeared, dragging down a link or two of gut, inch by slow inch. The dry part of the cast floated down, and I waited with that breathless expectancy which fishermen know so well. Then there was an almost imperceptible pull at the gut, a drawing of it over the polished surface, so slight that it might be due only to the quicker sinking of the fly, as the fish took me under water. I saw it, but saw it too late. I struck, but only pricked the fish, and with a swirl and a boil which showed how heavy he was he flounced off. Well, I ought to have caught that fish.

After that nothing happened for a long time. The mayfly got scarcer and scarcer, till at last it ceased altogether. The breeze dropped, not a leaf moved, and complete deadness fell on the water. So calm was the air, so peaceful the river, that it was difficult to believe that mayfly would ever return or that the active bustling trout would ever rise at them. I sat under a willow, ate my sandwiches, and sat under a willow again. Reed warblers and sedge warblers chattered on the bank, larks sang, and a pair of redshanks swept past, uttering their querulous cry. At last, at three o'clock, a solitary mayfly appeared, followed by two or three, then more, then thicker and thicker, till finally I realised that I should witness that wonderful sight, a great hatch. Soon the water was covered, and the air full. They settled on my coat, on my hat, and on my rod. Trout, already gorged on the nymph, rose spasmodically only, and it was difficult to find a feeding fish. At last I spotted one, greedier than the rest, taking every fly that came. He would not take me, however: I gave him several casts, with a winged artificial mayfly, and I confess they were soft casts and delicate, calculated to deceive the cunning, and my mayfly swung over him as light as a rose leaf. But he knew the difference between my fly and the natural, for he continued eating real mayfly, now to the right and to the left of my artificial. So I pulled in my line, and thought. An idea was running in my head. I nipped off my winged fly, and knotted on a hackled one, and did not oil it. The reason for this was to make it lie flat on the water. Since he would not take a fly which stood up like the real thing, let him have something quite different. I cast. My fly fell among a little drove of living flies, utterly unlike them: but the cunning old trout for that very reason seized it. I gave a firm pull and knew he was big. We had a long struggle, but, as often happens with big fish, not an active one. He weighed 2 pounds 4 ounces.

Then I found another, taking steadily and well, a big fish too. I gave him two or three casts, and then, through carelessness or ineptitude, I threw somewhat too hard and the fly went down on the water with a bang. That finished that trout: he stopped rising. I finally settled down for another. I had on the same fly; and though he refused it time after time, I did not change it, for I had a feeling that if he took anything he would take that. And so he did, but not till nearly an hour had passed. At last he took, and away he went upstream, the reel screaming. We had a long, slogging fight, but in the end I lost him through folly. He was dead beat. I was impatient, I tried to pull him over the net, and pulled too hard. The hook came away. He was very large, alas, alas.

Almost immediately after I caught one more. Now this fish would not look at the hackle fly; and instead of persevering with it as I did with the last fish, I at once changed it for a winged one. I did so because I put him down to be an individual of less astuteness and experience than the one I had just lost, and so for him an exact copy of the fare that he was eating was the best lure. The other trout, who had seen many exact copies of many flies and known their deceitfulness, was too superlatively wily to be taken in. No winged fly could pass his critical and dispassionate inspection, sharpened as it was by a continual view of the living article. No, give him something that had not to pass the test of comparison, and thus counter his extreme craftiness by apparent simplicity.

I caught one more, and then it was time to go home for a meal. I did not get back to the river till eight o'clock. On an evening such as this, fair and sweet, cloudless and windless, it was certain that the dead mayfly, the spent gnat, would be floating down the water, and there is no food of which trout are greedier. I started on a broad racing shallow, and at once a fish rose close under some bushes. I hooked him, and like most fish hooked on a shallow, he made a wild rush for deep water, in this case above him, and my reel was run down to the backing before I could stop him. Next he tried to dive head first into various thick beds of weed, but

was frustrated and finally landed. I strolled up, with that delightful feeling that whatever happened the day was redeemed. I had caught two brace. If I got more, it would be an added satisfaction; if I did not, it would cause no discontent.

It was a long time before the next fish moved. He was in the deep water at the head of the shallow, he rose only once when I was some way off and then not again. But I thought I knew where he was, and after waiting a bit I began to get out line to cast over him. As I was lengthening my throw, and was resting my fly on the water some 2 yards below where I imagined him to be, a fish took with a splash and was firmly hooked. But he did not play strongly and when I saw him I was not surprised to find him undersized. Was this my fish? It is uncommonly hard to mark a rise when you are 20 or 30 yards below, and I might easily have been some distance out. Yes, I suppose it was. I half reeled up, preparing to move on, when a subconscious thought forced itself to the front. It said, think again; think of the rise you first saw: picture it in your mind; was that, could it have been, caused by the miserable pounder you have just returned? Think again, it said, and then cast again 2 yards higher. I lengthened my line, and was rewarded by a rise that made my heart glad. He weighed 2½ pounds.

By now dusk had come on, stars were in the sky and in the air bats had taken the place of swifts. All was over.

A wonderful day truly. Five trout, the smallest 2 pounds exactly, and the biggest 3 pounds 4 ounces. Was there ever such a sport as fishing, or such a river as the Test? Going home, recalling the incidents of the day, all seemed symbolic. The very mistakes and misfortunes had their place and their necessity. And from the back of the mind, unobserved during the intense drama of the sport but returning with the cessation of activity, there arose a deep consciousness of the beauty of the background against which the contest had been enacted. The ageless outline of the down, springing from a time far earlier than man and man's cultivations, the grass with its wealth of flowers, the song of birds, the glancing water – all this entered into the inner chamber of the soul, giving a refreshment, a poise, a balance and a new life to intellect and to emotions which no other experience could offer.

John Waller Hills

The Harvest Moon

I had always believed that chalk-stream trout did not rise at night. You can catch them after dark, of course, and many of them: but this is merely the prolongation of the evening rise, not a night rise proper, which is a distinct event, starting later, above all starting after an interval, usually of one or two hours. I was quite certain that, the evening rise once ended, trout did not begin again, and that you did not get in Hampshire that second movement which takes place on some waters, where, in the opal dusk of a northern summer, you can fish from midnight till dawn. And of all evenings I should have considered one with a full moon the very worst. A full moon behind your arm was fatal as I had proved, and even in front of us was bad. Trout are far more shy by moonlight than by sunlight. From this I concluded that there was no real moonlight rise on the Test. Thus I committed that facile mistake, generalising from knowledge which though true was incomplete. Moreover, you should not generalise about fishing, which admits not of generalisation. I was to learn something that evening of which I was ignorant before, for all my angling years.

As we walked to the river, the fisherman and I, in the chill September twilight, I asked the usual question about the prospect of sport. He answered that I should be lucky to catch anything at the ordinary evening rise, but that if I liked to stay out till ten o'clock, I was sure to do well. Then, after a pause, he added: 'It's full moon tonight, harvest moon.'

For a moment, the force of his words did not penetrate. It is such a commonplace among Hampshire fishermen that there is no night fishing, and that a full moon is much worse than a cloudless sun, that my brain refused to accept them. But, when I had recovered, the old fisherman quietly told me that once a year, at full moon of the harvest moon, trout would rise, though no other moon suited them equally well. I was silent, too astonished to enquire further.

As predicted, nothing happened during the first hour. One or two fish moved in that languid and spasmodic manner which they adopt when they do not intend to be caught. Then they stopped altogether, and I reeled up and waited for the moon. The sky cleared, it got colder and there was a light draught of air from the north. At last a glow in the east announced the rising of the moon, and she swung up over the dark wood, silvering all the world. We had been on the east bank, looking into such light as remained from where the sun had set: we now crossed over so as to fish right into the moonlight. The river was broad, 20 to 30 yards, flowing at a sharp even pace, its surface luminous like quicksilver. I waited, still sceptical, but well content to watch the pure, cold beauty of the autumn night. But not for long did I wait.

Suddenly a trout rose in mid-stream, and the waves of his rise, widening over the river and catching the moonlight as they moved, were made visible as by day, turning the surface into a mass of shivering spangles. I cast over him, hooked him, he plunged across the stream and got off. Another fish moved right under the far bank. It was a long cast even by daylight, and I was doubtful whether I could reach him, for a long throw requires accurate timing, and it is hard to judge rightly when you cannot see your line. But there was no difficulty. Throwing over 20 yards, I could yet plainly see my gut before it fell on the water, glistening like the scale of a herring, with iridescent drops streaming from it: ay, and I could see my fly too, floating gaily on the surface. It was no doubt a big one, a hackle sedge: but it was 25 yards off, and yet there it was, plain and obvious. For some time the trout went on rising, keeping the surface all in a quiver of pearly light but disregarding my fly, so I changed to a cinnamon sedge, a size bigger. This he had at once, with a mighty wallop, and was soon in the net. Trout never fight hard at night, and very rarely go to weed. He weighed 2 pounds exactly.

As the moon rose higher the night became clearer and colder. We walked slowly upstream. In a stretch shaded by heavy trees a trout splashed, and I peered into the wall of darkness to find him. At first, turning from the white moonlight into the dark obscurity of the trees, I could see nothing. But after a time the shadow became liquid, the darkness was made visible, and I could make out a faint movement on the black velvet of the water. I cast, but in the inky shadow it was impossible to see whether the fly went right. The wind, too, began to blow more strongly, straight downstream. At last the fish appeared to come at me, but only half-heartedly; he was not hooked, and stopped rising. We moved up higher still. Here the prospect widened, opening out into a broad stretch of level land, with the tiled roofs of the village and the slate steeple of the church on the one hand and a tall oblong mill on the other. The valley lay silent and still under the dominance of the moon, and river and reeds, meadows and distant woods were drenched in her clean and lucid light. So cold and hard was this light, so different was the atmosphere from the gracious warmth of a summer dusk, that a rise seemed unthinkable. Yet it was not so. Two or three trout were moving regularly, making ripples of silver phosphorescence. One of them, lying in mid-stream, took my sedge quietly and well, but, struck too soon, was missed, and flounced off with a splash. The next was almost touching the opposite bank, another long cast, and in a channel surrounded by weeds. After some failures – it was a narrow target – he was hooked, and hauled successfully over the weeds, protesting vigorously, into the clear water, but there he too came off.

By then it was past ten o'clock, our fingers were cold, and as the trout appeared to have retired to the bottom, we all went home to a fireside. I had only caught one, but I had had a chance of five. Above all, I had gained an experience.

Vincent C. Marinaro

A Game of Nods

T here is an older generation of fishermen, to which I belong, who have memories of a special kind of pleasure, not evident today. Those memories belong to the days of pure silk lines and silkworm gut leaders, when preparations for a day's fishing involved a special kind of ritual, religiously observed. The day always began with the stretching, cleaning and greasing of the pure silk lines that would not float well, undressed. Then came the sorting and examining of the silkworm gut leaders to choose one suitable for the conditions of that day and perhaps to add a new tippet or two, after which the leader needed to be soaked and softened for a considerable length of time to make it pliant.

All this required some time and a satisfactory location. There was such a place, on the bank, beside the Letort – a lovely, grassy, sun-drenched spot, lush and soft to sit upon – and there I went at the beginning of each fishing day to prepare my tackle in the many little ways now cherished only in memory.

Close to the bank where I sat, and just a little off the main current, there was a little eddy that caught much of the flotsam coming downriver and held it interminably while it spun around very slowly. This was an interesting eddy, because in it lived a very interesting trout.

I became aware of him one fine summer morning while I was in the midst of preparing my tackle and, as always, with one eye on the river. There was that tiny little bulge in the surface film, a faint dividing of the current and a little circular ripple expiring with the flow of the quiet water. I saw it out of the corner of an eye, my fringe vision if you please, which no fly-fisherman should neglect to cultivate assiduously.

The next time he rose I was prepared for him so that I was able to see and locate his home and his riseform. I did not know it at the time but this trout had a name. In fact, I myself christened him and called him 'the Untouchable.' But this happened a long time afterward, when I had made many hundreds of casts and had suffered as many refusals.

At first it was a very friendly contest. Even so, his refusals astonished me a little. I rationalised my failures with the thought that I was not really trying to catch him. Anyway, he was a likeable fellow. I did not want to discourage his presence in the eddy and I wanted him to be a part of my little ceremony of preparation on the soft grassy, sun-drenched bank near his home. I continued to make my futile casts to him; then, upon being refused, I tipped the long bill of my fishing cap in a silent tribute to his shrewdness and went my way to seek a more gullible breed of trout.

Eventually the contest began to take on a grimmer aspect and with it, finally, came the sombre realisation that this trout could not be taken, not by me. On the morning of that realisation the well-prepared tackle was laid aside, and I made no more casts, for now I had to watch his every move and discover, perhaps, why he defeated me and why I had failed. He had humbled me, this trout of the eddy. His refusals were as eloquent as the spoken word. So began my long vigil while the trout of the eddy continued to flirt his tail and make his darting upward rises entirely unconcerned with my resentment and my watchful waiting.

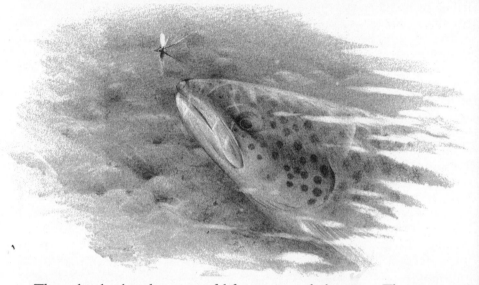

Then, bit by bit, his way of life was revealed to me. There was no blinding flash of revelation. There were only bits and scraps of information to be sorted and related and evaluated. There was, however, one outstanding fact to be considered more than anything else. He turned out to be an individualist, a kind of gourmet among trout, because this trout ate only one kind of insect which he, invariably, chose among the many displayed for his pleasure on the travelling dinner table near his eddy. What was this one insect? Was it one of the breed of aristocratic mayflies to which all trout are extraordinarily addicted? Or was it one of the bourgeois family of terrestrials born and bred in one of the rich meadows bordering the Letort? No, it was none of these. It was, of all things, a common housefly!

He ate them in enormous quantities, all day long, day after day. Their presence on the water in large numbers was a bit of a mystery until I traced the fly-bearing current upstream to the most obvious housefly source in all the world – namely, the dung heaps of a barnyard on the bank adjacent to the water. There was a convenient watering place too, where cattle were accustomed to linger, switching contentedly at house-flies during the hot summer days. A housefly is not to be scorned because of these associations. After all, he must and should rank with mushrooms and other delectable gourmet foods with a similar lowly origin.

It was plain then that I must cause the downfall of the trout in the eddy with an imitation of the housefly. Nothing else would do! So I tied houseflies and houseflies. I made many casts with those flies and continued to get nothing but refusals. My most artful imitations were of no avail and even a few secret incantations supplementing my casts and practised only in dire emergencies, amounted to nothing but idle gestures.

Again the well-prepared tackle was laid aside and again I watched this fellow more intently than ever before, but now I saw something new to consider. The trout in the eddy did not eat all the houseflies that paraded before him. Many were taken, it is true, but many were rejected even after the most careful inspection in that manner peculiar to the trout – his nose barely touching the insect, undulating backward with the current, frowning-frowning, finally accepting or rejecting the offering as it pleased him.

Now I knew that the trout in the eddy must be ignored; instead, the housefly must be watched to discover why it was often rejected by the trout. A housefly is a very interesting creature. He has some very unusual gifts and habits. Aerodynamically, he is some kind of an oddity – a biological freak. He isn't supposed to be able to do the things that he can do. The laws of inertia were certainly not made for him. From a standing start without any visible windup he can take off with blinding speed without the need for gradual acceleration. It is a mystery why houseflies do not leave their wings behind, torn from their bodies, by the terrific counterforces generated by that amazing takeoff. Moreover, he lands the same way. It is very difficult to follow him in flight; only when he is hovering or buzzing in tight little circles can we see him well. He also has another odd characteristic: he can remain absolutely immobile and lifeless in appearance like a 'painted fly on a painted river', to paraphrase a famous quote.

Finally, in desperation, as the last measure of my resources, I began to play a game of nods. It is something that I invented many years ago. In those days when all the logical steps had been taken, when my reasoning, inductive or deductive, failed to achieve a successful dry-fly imitation, that game of nods was the last resort. The game is played by tying a reasonable facsimile of the insect being taken by the trout. Then many variations of this basic pattern are tied with only slight differences in each of them. These are in turn cast to a visible feeding trout, and his reaction noted very carefully. A trout has different ways of showing his interest in a fly. He may, when the fly is seen, suddenly begin to accelerate his fins, lifting his head for a brief instant, then suddenly drop to his original position. Or, if the fly is cast to the right or left of the trout, he may nod sideways, briefly toward the fly indicating his interest. Or, if his interest is really aroused, the nod may become a leisurely movement that puts him under the fly to drift with it and inspect it very carefully. Each fly is cast as long as it receives a nod from the trout. When it no longer excites any nods it is discarded for a new variation, each of them being rated for the number of nods. At the end of the game all the highest rated variations are combined into one desirable and perhaps successful pattern.

It was in this fashion that I played the game of nods with the trout of the eddy and finally, one late summer day, my efforts were rewarded. He slid under one of my housefly patterns, put his nose under it and drifted backward with it, frowning-frowning, while I trembled a little from the realisation that free float was about to end and drag begin. Suddenly he made up his mind, lifted and sucked the fly. Exultant, I lifted the rod tip, felt the resistance for a moment, then it was gone and the fly popped out of the water to drift aimlessly along the ground. I had a brief glimpse of the trout streaking away for cover. At times like this it is best to just sit quietly for a while, to just stare at things – the sky, the water, trees, flowers – and have no serious thoughts of any kind. The hiatus, occupied by his reverie, will prepare the fisherman for a calm appraisal and judicial thought. So I came out of my reverie, picked up the successful fly, and looked at it very carefully. It had a thin body of unstripped peacock quill and a wing made by tying pale bluish hackle fibres flat over the body and clipped at the rear to make a flat glassy wing like a housefly at rest. There was something else. At the head of the fly there were three long glinting alert-looking hackle fibres and as I stared at these the light of understanding began to glimmer and glow, faintly at first, then with increasing brilliance. I knew now why some houseflies were taken and some were rejected. I lifted the fly toward my lips and I blew gently on the fibres – blew from the sides, blew rear and front. I blew from above and below. Then I put the fly in the palm of my hand and rocked it gently and with every puff of wind, every little rock, the three glassy alert fibres trembled and nodded and quivered to resemble the only movement I had forgotten in the housefly's catalogue of characteristics, namely, his ancient habit, no matter how still or lifeless he may appear to be, of lifting and rubbing together his two forefeet! This was the sign that the trout of the eddy looked for. From that day forward all my houseflies wore antennae, never fewer than two, never more than three.

In the succeeding years, the housefly incident acquired an increasingly greater significance in my mind, particularly because it gave me a new approach in appraising the efficacy of fly patterns. I continued to play the game of nods and in doing so came to appreciate those occasions when a particular pattern would bring a trout up to make a repeated inspection. When you have done that much you have gone a long way in devising a successful imitation and you are very close to the secret of what imitation really is.

George Melly

There's More Than One Rise

nyone walking up Charing Cross Road during the month of August may catch the sound of what would appear to be a very large moth-grub chewing its way through a drawer full of cashmere sweaters. It is in fact our agent, Jolly Jack Higgins, frustratedly biting lumps out of his wall-to-wall carpeting. In August John Chilton, the Feetwarmers and myself insist, despite whatever grossly subtle offers he dangles in front of us, on taking *a whole month's holiday.*

This year the last gig is in Shropshire, an out-of-doors engagement for which the weather has decided to be kind. A warm and mothy night on the flat top of a steep hill behind a charming pub; a stage, rickety but adequate, facing a beer-tent; the smell of a roasting sheep, and a large and, in part, increasingly legless audience on the crushed, sweet-scented grass under the starry sky.

It's a very charming way to break up, and the presence in the audience of my wife Diana, my son Tom, and a friend with three children indicates that we are within easy driving distance of the Welsh Tower where Diana spends her summers and I whatever time I can, including the thirty days to come. At the end of the evening we totter down the hill. The Feetwarmers head for their hotel in Leominster and our party for the Brecon Beacons.

The Tower is not as grand as it sounds. It is quite a small tower built by the Normans; one of a series along the Welsh marches into which they could retreat to fire arrows at the early Welsh nationalists when the going got rough. In the seventeenth century somebody knocked off the castellations and put on a roof. They built three floors and smashed their way through 6 foot thick walls to install some predictably askew windows. There's Diana's vegetable garden and a bit of a moat and it lies in a basin of green hills with the river Usk meandering around it in a curve a few hundred yards away. The perfect antidote to the motels in which I spend so many of my nights.

The Usk is for me the centre of my Welsh life as it is full of large and capricious trout and I have a rod on the water. I'm also an 'important' bore when it comes to fishing. Successful or unsuccessful I return each evening unable to stop myself describing triumph or disaster, the changing of flies, the depth and coloration of the river, the difficulty

of covering certain pools when the wind is in a particular quarter. My family and our guests snigger or yawn according to mood and temperament, but I can't help myself. Any fisherman among my readers will understand.

The days are almost identical: writing, fishing, eating, sleeping. There are friends to be collected or returned to Abergavenny or Newport, the occasional shopping expedition to Brecon or Crickhowell. The beetroot has done well. Carrot fly has struck. There are two horror films to watch on Saturday nights.

This year, however, and on my birthday to boot, there is the promise of considerable sophistication and excitement. In Cardiff, all of 50 miles away, I've been asked to join the Mayor and other dignitaries in judging 'Miss Moped – Wales', a semi-final of the 'Miss Moped – Great Britain' competition, organized by *Practical Moped* magazine, a journal, I must admit, unknown to me until fairly recently, but, in recent months, very much a part of my life. The editor wrote to me initially to solicit an article. Having a great deal of work to do and not wishing to offend, I wrote back, to an address in North London, agreeing in principle but asking for what I imagined to be too stiff a fee. Not a bit of it. They accepted without quibbling, I scribbled off my experiences as a moped driver of some ten years' standing and Marilyn, my secretary, told me, only a week later, that with a promptness that many a more distinguished journal might follow, the cheque had arrived and been paid in. By the same post another letter. The editor understood I had a cottage in Wales. Was it within 'moped-riding distance of Cardiff' and if so was I prepared to help judge 'Miss Moped – Wales' on the evening of 17 August? Would I also consider taking out the runner-up, 'at our expense of course' for an evening 'on the town'?

I rang Diana. It might be fun to be a judge: 'General standard of handling, ability to effect minor repairs, appearance', and we could then have dinner together in Cardiff. She agreed immediately. On the other hand I decided to turn down my role as second prize. 'The ability to effect minor repairs' might lead to a bumpy evening, especially as I have to take my Maxi-Puch into Chamberlaine's every time it has a flat.

A week later the editor of *Practical Moped* rang me up in person. Speaking in a technological voice, he asked me if I would be willing to be photographed in the saddle. I agreed to an appointment, making certain it would clash with another date to be photographed accepting delivery of the new bandwagon, and another wearing a monocle.

It may strike the reader unconnected with show-biz that the whole affair was getting out of hand, but it didn't surprise me. Only a month or two before I had appeared on the cover of the *Home Organist*, and they had not only interviewed me at length, but actually installed a compact but extremely heavy organ in the sitting room so that I could be photographed with one hand hovering over the keys. At least I owned a moped.

Unfortunately the moped photographer was 'indisposed' on the day of our appointment, but they accepted the use of the cover of *It's George*, an LP on which I am seen mounted and in motion, and I asked Marilyn to send it express.

I got one more letter, this time in Wales. To accommodate the Mayor would I object to a lunchtime judging? I wrote back that it would be perfectly agreeable. Diana and I could have lunch in one of Cardiff's more fashionable Italian bistros. The morning of the seventeenth dawned overcast and muggy. And the fish were rising noisily!

Diana then announces that she is not feeling very well but that Pam Spinks, a friend in the neighbourhood, has volunteered to take me instead. I ask Tom and my step-daughter Candy who has arrived in the interim, if they would like to come. They declined wholeheartedly.

Pam and her son Ed are there in plenty of time and we set off. A mile or two along the way Ed announces that he feels car-sick. At my suggestion we drive back to deposit him at the Tower. I see the fish are still rising and agree to take him in while Pam turns the car around in the narrow lane. At the door Diana meets me, listens to my explanation, and says that anyway it's just as well I came back as Jack Higgins is on the phone and it's urgent. I rush in, musn't keep the Mayor waiting, and grab the receiver. A girl's voice, with a slight Welsh lilt, tells me about the weather. Have I or Jack Higgins gone mad?

Behind me the sounds of suppressed hysteria. I turn round. Candy, wearing a 'Miss Moped – Wales' sash, is seated on Tom's Maxi-Puch which they've carried into the kitchen, while its owner is rolling about on the floor. I stare out of the window to regain my composure and see the trout are still rising like crazy things. It slowly penetrates my confusion that the whole thing is an elaborate hoax.

At first I can't believe it. 'What about the letters?' Typed by Marilyn, whose address was at the top. They knew I wouldn't remember where she lived. 'But the cheque?' Had I seen it? Had I looked at my bank statement? 'But the editor on the phone?' An actor friend.

So there is no *Practical Moped*, at least not a real one, but Diana and the children have gone to immense trouble to produce a single issue. Candy did the drawings and most of the writing, including hot fashion tips from Paris, New York and Milan, and helmets designed by students at the Royal College of Art: 'the snail', 'the monster' and 'hair', permed or straight. The dullest thing in the whole 'issue' is my article, written for gain, and shamingly stapled in.

Among other spin-offs was a photograph of Louis Armstrong sprouting a bubble reading 'Dat honky singer sho' has been dooped'. Satch, you never spoke a truer word!

I look outside towards the river. The trout have stopped rising.

Geoffrey Palmer

The Brigadier Floats By

I have always loved rivers, even before I took up fishing comparatively recently. The sea frightens me, but fresh running water has always held a certain magic for me. And fishing rivers has so many joys: peace and tranquillity, the sight of your prey below or above the water's surface, the take, the strike, the play, the glimpse of a kingfisher or the quiet watching of a dipper, a water vole, or a weasel. Just being there, really.

Normally, I am something of am antisocial creature and so one of the less obvious pleasures of fishing for me has been some of the people I have met. And from all the other fishermen, keepers, boatmen and ghillies I have come across, one gentleman stands out.

I found myself for the first time on the Tulchan stretch of the middle Spey, looking beyond the Scots firs and the impressive wild cherry trees to the Hills of Cromdale, remembering that the further glen is named Livet. This incomparable setting was intoxicating enough in itself but add the river, pool after pool of good salmon-holding water, and I understood why the Spey attracts anglers from far and wide. After a fruitless morning on D Beat and, as a newcomer, feeling intimidated by ghillies, other rods, even the river itself, I made my way along to A Beat for lunch.

'A Bloody Mary, Sir, or a dry Martini before lunch?' asked Joe, the liveried butler, as the waitresses bustled about. I suppose about ten or twelve of us sat down for lunch. On my right was a guest of one of the other rods staying at Tulchan Lodge. He was there only for the one day but had fished all over Scotland for many, many years.

As lunch went on – 'A little more claret, Sir?' – I admitted that, never having waded before, I was a bit scared with what felt like most of the Spey pushing me in the small of the back.

'Oh, my dear fellow, you mustn't be,' said my companion. 'I mean, I've been under several times and I'm still here.'

'Well, you must be a helluva good swimmer,' I replied.

'No, can't swim a stroke. Couldn't at Eton, couldn't at Sandhurst. Still can't!'

'What do you do, then?'

'I just lie there and paddle a bit and you end up on the bank sometime.'

'But people drown!' I said.

'Yes, I've lost a few chums over the years.'

'Oh, really?' I was not feeling any less nervous but it was a good lunch and my companion was still smiling and giving the impression that a ducking was all part of the fun. 'On the Spey?' I asked.

'Oh, yes, here on the Spey. Mind you, I don't think any of them were straight drownings, you know.'

'Straight drownings?' I queried, finishing my claret.

'Mmm! They were either pissed or had suffered heart attacks, I think. Possibly both!'

'Oh, I see . . .'

He then recounted a story of when, many years earlier, he had been fishing a beat further upstream and was lunching with the head ghillie who looked at his watch and said, 'The Brigadier should be coming past soon.' Apparently, the Brigadier, quite aged and a connoisseur of mature single malts, would fall in and float past quite frequently before beaching himself in one of several chosen spots.

My companion's next question really astonished me: 'You live in the south; tell me – do they still have the rat shoots in the basements of some of those London stores on Sunday mornings?' By now transfixed, I replied that I would not have thought so but did not honestly know. 'Oh, they were great fun. Just after the war. Some very good shots, you know, used to meet at nine o'clock. Sweep through the basement. Bang, bang, bang. A few drinks, then home for lunch.'

Rather sadly, the time came to return to D Beat, where I got nowhere near a salmon that afternoon, or for the rest of that week. But I had had a memorable time and for one wonderful lunch had enjoyed the company of a man, as attractive a personality as you could hope to meet, of rare charm and style, and a great raconteur. A sort of David Niven with a touch of Rex Harrison.

I am very glad I took up fishing.

Tony Pawson

Madman's Pool

For me there was an early lesson about the power of big fish. My father was in the Sudan Civil Service and, aged four, I was taken to one of the Nile dams where a fishing party was being held. For my amusement someone asked me to hold his line while he fetched food from his car. Aigel, or Nile perch, can run to hundreds of pounds and one chose to hook itself a moment later. It towed me over the rocks and into the river's edge before I let go. So it is no fisherman's tale to say that the first fish I hooked was so large it caught me!

We always remember the fish that get away more than those we catch, especially if we think they are large but have not actually seen them. I have imagined this aigel as being as enormous as the one my brother once described in a letter to me from Khartoum soon after the war: 'I set off one morning to do some dawn shooting for sandgrouse in the desert. As we drove along the embankment beside the Blue Nile, close to the Omdurman Bridge, I noticed a great white object blocking the road ahead. It was a Nile perch just hauled ashore by a huge night-line. We measured it at approximately 8 feet in length and estimated its weight at over 300 pounds. The captor soon returned in a taxi to take it to the Khartoum fish *suk* [market]. Aigel are delicious to eat and usually the main course on Sudan railways. Fish of 200 pounds are not unusual but this one was special!'

My mother, fishing in Lake No, would have had a story to tell of losing one of this size had it got away. Unfortunately, she landed it with help from my father and it turned out to be the decaying hindquarters of a hippopotamus!

Before dismissing these as typical anglers' exaggerations, bear in mind what happened in a pool of the river Towy. Compared to the Nile this is a tiny salmon and sea trout stream in Wales where I have had some magical night fishing, especially in its tributary, the Cothi. But on 25 September 1933 Mr A.L. Allen and a friend set off from the local pub for an evening's fishing in the White Mill pool a few miles above Carmarthen, using small spinners for sea trout. In the dark, Allen's line stuck solid in an immovable object. When the fish eventually surged off he imagined a record salmon, as something huge then stranded itself in the shallows. In fact, his spinner had hooked in the back of a sturgeon which had almost filled the pool. It was 9 feet 3 inches long and weighed 388 pounds. As a sturgeon is a royal fish, Allen telegraphed to the king, who waived his right. So they sold it in Carmarthen market for £5, not a great price had it also been full of caviare! But had they returned to the pub with a tale of a monster lost, who would have believed the story of this much-photographed and well-documented fish?

My mother might have had a similarly unbelievable tale to tell had she lost a salmon hooked on a prawn in the boat pool of the Tyrcellyn beat of the Welsh Wye below Builth Wells. In this case the disbelief would have been justified, despite the tale being honest. Here too the dusk was fading into dark when the salmon was hooked and mother could make no impression on the fish despite maximum pressure. Father was boatman and finally took over the rod. As extra pressure was applied what looked in the gloaming like a large horn appeared above the surface. A startled father let the mysterious creature drop back to the depths. Fifteen minutes later the riddle was solved as he gaffed a 10-pound salmon which had swum through a rusting bottomless bucket, which had added to the difficulties of playing it. The broken handle of the bucket looked like a horn in the gathering dark as it broke the surface first.

No real or suspected monsters have taken my fly, but the largest salmon I have lost and the largest I have caught both gave me problems in plenty. The largest I ever hooked was in the clear waters of the Laerdal in Norway, on the bottom beat where it runs into the fjord. It was August and the river was noted for large salmon and large sea trout. Mainly I fished for sea trout through a night illuminated by the pale glow of the midnight sun. With sea trout up to 12 pounds keeping the reel screaming as they careered away in the fast water, this was thrilling stuff indeed. But at that late time of the season all the salmon were supposed to have passed through this beat.

After repairing to the hostel beside the river for a few hours' sleep I started one morning to walk up the river bank to the boat in order to row to the fishing hut on the opposite bank. All I had was my rod, made up for the previous night's sea trout fishing with three size 8 flies on a 7-pound cast. As I passed one croix I saw a sea trout swirl and immediately cast in its area. That fish, or its companion, promptly took and a 4-pound sea trout was lost as I was trying to net it with my ordinary walking shoes slipping about on the wet stones of the croix. After uttering some mild expletive, I cast again and this time there was a huge swirl and a salmon of around 40 pounds went porpoising up the main current of the long pool. Unfortunately it then played doggo and with that strength of cast, weakened by the droppers, there was a limit to the pressure I could apply. Three hours later I had at last manouevred it into slacker water below me and even got the top dropper above the surface.

However, my kind host had made it quite clear that Norwegian hospitality made it impossible for him to leave before the fight was over, but he had also told me he had to fly back for an important business meeting. By this time, therefore, he was looking at his watch every five minutes. Had I been alone I would have played it all day, if necessary, but I responded to this pressure with too much pressure on the fish in a 'land or bust effort' – which ended in bust.

My wealthy host departed on a chartered sea-plane – of which I was glad to see the last. When we had boarded it in Oslo a week earlier a near gale had been blowing and there was something of an altercation between my host and the two pilots. As he regained his seat and reverted to English, Arild said: 'Two of the best pilots in Norway and they say it is too dangerous to take off. I have told them to get on with it!' My eyes were firmly closed at take-off and again when flying over a range of bare, spiky mountains with, it seemed, a few feet to spare and the pilot leaning out to wipe off some oil that was spattering the windscreen.

My second largest salmon was a 27-pound fish in Iceland. There, too, the flight to the river gave me a collywobble or two. The trip had been arranged by my doctor, who was also a leading ornithologist and a regular visitor to Iceland where he studied the harlequin ducks, the only ones to prefer living in fast currents. As a regular visitor he had asked the head of Iceland Air in England to organise some fishing for me. This he had done with two keen anglers among the airline's pilots accompanying me to a river in the north. We met at Reykjavik, with my tickets entitling me to fly to the northern capital, Akureri, then go by bus to Husavik. My new friends laughed at that, said the pilot was a friend of theirs and, ticket or no ticket, we would fly on to Husavik. That entailed a flight around the coastline landing at intervals at 'airports' which seemed to consist of windsocks flying above lava strips. So it was with considerable relief that I made for the exit after a bumpy landing at Husavik. But I was commanded to sit down again with the daunting news: 'The pilot's a friend so he will land us by the fishing hut.' Which he did on a rutted lava road.

Two new problems then faced me. The fishing hut was in the middle of nowhere and stocked only with dried fish and horsemeat, both of which I found inedible. So I had to fish to survive on sea trout and the bilberries I found growing by the river. The second was that the river itself, though full of fish, was also full of floating wisps of weed which clung round the fly so that I had to wind in to clean the line and fly every few casts. I did not then know of a needle knot and when I played a salmon, the weed built up around the knot until I was also playing a football of weed. This cost me the first five salmon I hooked and I was still coming to terms with it when I hooked the large one. By the time I had exhausted it and myself, the football was so large that the rod was bent double playing it with the salmon wiggling behind. Only when the salmon unwisely floated within range was I able to grab it by the tail.

The heaviest I caught was a 30-pounder in the Brora river in Sutherland. The river was in flood, fining down but still coloured. As sea trout were also plentiful I had two droppers on the cast, but it was the tail fly that was seized. In the heavy water it took me more than half an hour to get the salmon under control, with the two droppers out of the water. Then, however, it took off again in what I hoped was a final dash to the far end of the long pool. There I turned it on the edge of some rapids and walked it back up to safety. To my surprise I could no longer get even the top dropper out of the water, and was even more astounded when a tip of its tail appeared. In turning, the fish's tail had hooked the top dropper and I was now playing a 30-pounder as if foul-hooked, albeit tired. At that moment the bailiff arrived and offered to net it for me. Happy to agree I passed him my net, warning him that large as the net itself was, the handle was a thin wooden one and no attempt should be made to hoist the fish out. Fifteen minutes later the fish was played out but the bailiff made a series of missed nettings, not realising where the head and body were in the murky water. Over-excited, when he finally got it into the net he yanked it up with some wild Scottish cry – and the handle snapped in pieces. At that I dived in head first and recovered the net-head, happily with the salmon safely in it still.

'What is this pool called?' I asked as I recovered my breath.

'The Madman's – and that was before *You* came here!'

Datus Proper

Conversations With Trout

(On Imitations, Fancy Flies, Lures, and How to Tell the Difference)

T rout can settle most angling arguments. But they don't know much about art; they just know what they like. And you have to be a good listener, because they are bashful. Anglers, on the contrary, have been shouting back and forth at each other for a few hundred years. It's hard to filter out the noise and pick up a faint whisper from the depths of running water.

Trout get through to me sometimes. I am not boasting about it. By comparison to fishermen, trout are pretty sober. But reliable.

I started receiving fishy messages at a tender age. In those days, I was inclined to argue back, so the conversations did not last long. There were lots of trout near my home in Yellowstone Park, and I could always find a stupid one. Then I got old enough to drive. The fertile Firehole River tempted me with bigger fish. They were also smarter, and they made me listen. A few years later the trout of the Pennsylvania spring creeks had a lot to say.

But for really talkative creatures, you should listen to Irish browns. The accent can be a bit thick. The gillaroos from Mayo lose me entirely, though of course I never let on. The fat trout of the limestone midlands come through clearly. And they seldom stop talking; they have such great material to work with.

In Pennsylvania, by the time the trout have started to learn something about Hendricksons, the hatch is gone; it usually peaks on one Wednesday and Thursday while I am a hundred miles away earning my wages, and then a heavy rain floods the river Saturday. In Ireland, I can count on a perfect hatch of Large Dark Olives by St Patrick's Day, and the hatch is still going on in May. By then there are also the Grey Flag sedge, the Iron Blue Dun, and the Black Gnat, just to mention the durable hatches. Best of all is the Blue-Winged Olive, which you can fish every fine evening from June through September. The trout learn something about these flies, with hooks or without, and they will tell you. To be sure you are getting the right message, make just one small change in your fly between trips. Then, if you really listen to what the trout say instead of to what you want to believe, you can draw some conclusions about fly design. And that is the story of this book.

My first 'imitation' of the Large Dark Olives was trout-proof. I tied it from a pattern. It was too big, too bushy, and entirely the wrong colour; but most of the changes it needed were obvious. Four seasons later, my olives were pretty respectable. Mind you, I'm just repeating the trout's opinion. I've said nothing.

The Blue-Winged Olive – a different genus – was more difficult. The trout told me clearly that what looked right to me looked wrong to them. But they would not say what looked right. You may think the Irish are forthcoming, but it's a cover. They hide the important things.

So there I was one August day, up to my unmentionables in the Kells Blackwater. The Irish never wade that deep, perhaps on principle, but I maintain that it is a good thing for unmentionables to keep them cool – something I read in Margaret Mead. Besides, wading is a good way to learn trout language.

This was a soft day, as they say in Ireland when it is about to rain buckets down your collar. A good day for hatches. And some 30 feet upstream, a trout was taking Blue-Winged Olive duns with a deep resonant swirl that made my fingers fumble. I tied on a fly that had worked once during a daytime Blue-Winged Olive hatch on a different river. She had a sleek blue-grey wing and a green-olive body – much like the natural female dun, to my eyes, and beautiful.

The trout told me that she was not beautiful. Not even vaguely interesting. The real duns, even bedraggled ones in pyjamas, kept disappearing with a ploop, which is strong language in troutese. My dun, all fancied up in a tight sweater, did not get a nod. Dumb trout.

So I tried a nymph, painstakingly copied from the monthly magazine that features Blue-Winged Olive nymphets. I greased my leader, except for the last few inches, and soaked the nymph in my mouth. It drifted down nicely, a few inches under water, on the first cast, and the second, and the third. Besides lacking in discernment, this trout was entirely defective in libido.

From Ned Maguire, standing on the bank, I thought I got a smirk, although it can be hard to tell through all the cigarette smoke. He had a big stupid brown fly on his leader. All right, if I couldn't get a rise out of the trout, I'd get one out of old Ned. I generously offered to let him try my fish, since I couldn't catch it and besides the disadvantage of his fly, he was in difficult casting position way up there on the bank.

From his awkward angle, he could not have got a long float, but he did not need one, because his fly lit a foot in front of the trout. Even from a distance, that fly was a real misfit, a tattooed weight-lifter among the ballet dancers. Yet the trout rose on the first float, with exactly the same ploop accorded the naturals.

'Ahaah' unless he feels the hook set solidly in a substantial weight. In this case, the substantial weight plunged upstream, leaving a visible furrow in the water, and shot into a mass of weeds. There are some refined methods for working on a weeded trout. I used the one that best suits my temperament – hot pursuit. Dreadfully untraditional. Fortunately, Ned's leader was stout, and the fish was well hooked in the corner of the mouth. I netted a 17-inch brown out of an underwater garden.

The reader will please note the scenario. Your eager author is now up to his armpits in river, holding a dripping net. The net contains a large, disconsolate trout and about a pickle-barrelful of weeds. On the bank is Ned, patched old hip-boots down around his knees and not quite the boy-o he used to be, he stood about five-seven and weighed 130 in wet tweeds.

My indisputable conclusion was that I had possession. I couldn't exactly run off with the trout, because Ned was driving, and it was a long walk home in waders. But Ned's leader was not nearly strong enough to pull me out till I had a good look at the fly and interviewed the trout.

The fly, besides being too big for a Blue-Winged Olive, had neither blue nor olive nor wings about it. It had a drab brown body of pheasant-tail herl ribbed with gold, plus a shiny, sparse hackle of mahogany red. This was, in fact, a well-known fancy fly, the Pheasant Tail Red Spinner.

The interview went like this:

AUTHOR: The jig is up, fishface. If you'd played my game, you might have got off with toothache. Instead you picked that smirking Irishman. Can you imagine him letting a fat, pink-fleshed trout swim away?
TROUT: (A visible shudder)
AUTHOR: Skip the dramatics. You have murdered mayflies by the score, to say nothing of sedges and shrimp. I want you to do the only decent thing in your life. In your last words, I want you to tell me why you, who must be intelligent to have lived so long, showed such bad taste in the end.
TROUT: Get yer t'umb outa me mout'.
AUTHOR: Sorry. I was looking at that fancy fly.
TROUT: You can keep yer sermons and yer Yankee accent and yer fancy flies. I never looked at a fancy fly since I was humiliated in me catechism. The fly that fought back just now looked like a hatching dun.
AUTHOR: Thanks, old man. Now here's Ned with the priest.
NED: Thunk!

A poignant exchange, you say, but not profound.

Consider, however, another quotation for which you do not have to take my word. In his excellent book entitled *Quill Gordon*, John McDonald says that 'both fancy and imitation flies take trout, but the reconciliation of the theories behind them would be the most revolutionary event in the history of fly-fishing. It would be easier to reconcile Plato and Aristotle.'

Ned's trout had just done the revolutionary reconciling. He cared nothing for theories, Plato, or Aristotle. But he had made clear that what we thought a fancy, he thought was food. And what I thought was an imitation, he thought was *not* food.

Now who do you want to believe, me or the trout? Even I point to the trout.

I am not claiming that every fly taken by a trout represents an imitation. That would be ridiculous. Trout eat salmon eggs, lures, Rat-Faced MacDougals, and some things I would hate to mention.

But when 'educated' trout, proven to be selective, consistently take a given artificial fly with the same rise-form they use for naturals, that fly must be considered an imitation. One trout would not establish that the Pheasant Tail Red Spinner imitates a Blue-Winged Olive. I later learned, however, that Ned was not just taking a random chance. Trout feeding on hatching Blue-Winged Olives will often take a pheasant tail body (which presumably looks like a nymph) with almost any hackle. If you ask me, such a fly is an imitation.

This point must be controversial, because such giants as Halford called flies imitative only when they looked good in *human* eyes. This is in fact the traditional approach. McDonald had reason to accept it. But it does not work very well.

Halford's final flies were described and illustrated in his *Modern Development of the Dry Fly*. I have some of the flies tied in his time after his patterns, and the odd thing is that they do not look like good imitations to me. They are the wrong shape (too heavily dressed) and often too big. Even the colours seem wrong, but that does not prove much, as colours of the naturals vary from river to river. The whole thing may simply demonstrate that different people in different ages see objects very differently. Anyone can satisfy himself on that score by walking through a museum and observing paintings from different periods and cultures.

Trout are not a bit interested in style – just survival. Food presumably looks the same to a trout today as to his ancestor centuries ago, though today's trout must look more carefully to be sure that the food is authentic. Drab old wet-fly patterns that were designed by experimentation to suit smart trout still work admirably. We still have the same old fish around to teach us humility and to puncture theories that have more to do with human culture than with mother nature.

Here we may need a parenthesis to explain the meaning of 'fancy flies'. The term is British, and Americans are often unaware that fancy does not mean gaudy. There is room for confusion, since some fancy flies also happen to be gaudy. Many others are sober creations that happen to be products of an *angler's* fancy. John Waller Hills says that a fancy fly may imitate insect life generally but cannot be 'connected with any particular species or genus or group'. By way of example, he gives Stewart's famous Black, Red and Dun Spiders, which are small, drab, wet flies for upstream fishing.

Hills then distinguishes fancy flies from 'general' flies, which 'imitate a genus or group, but not an individual'. The difference is a fine one. There is, however, a clear difference between fancy and general flies, on the one hand, and imitations of a specific insect, on the other. Or, to be more modest, we fishermen see a clear difference. Trout do not always agree.

Finally, to round out definitions, the British use the term 'lure' if the creation is designed only as an attractor, or if the creature imitated is not an insect. We Americans have never used this British definition, but it has one recommendation: the *trout* use it. They react in a special way to lures moved quickly in relation to the current, whether those lures are made of feathers, hair, or metal. Their response is more deliberate to flies, natural or artificial – including the flies we call fancies. Insects, and artificial flies representing them, can usually move only very slowly in relation to the current. Thus, by the trout's definition, streamers are certainly lures, and so are flies like the ancient Parmachene Belle. Henry Wells designed her to imitate a trout fin, not a fly.

So returning to John McDonald, fancy flies work for two reasons:

* They may not be fancies at all, but good imitations.
* Alternatively, *anything* would have worked, within reason.

The second alternative often applies, especially in America. The conditions for a selective rise may rarely be present in our fast streams, where you have to look harder for a hatch than for a trout.

There is no reason to apologize for using fancy flies. They are not like what the Victorians called fancy women. It is, however, futile to argue over the relative merits of, say, the Parmachene Belle and the Scarlet Ibis. They reflect human whims, not those of trout, and human whims are erratic, as anyone can see from comparing the plates of fancy flies in old books of different periods. Many a famous angler has promoted an all-purpose killer fly which has enjoyed a brief surge of popularity and faded with its author.

Imitative flies vary within much tighter limits. The trout holds us to account. Aldam's Black Gnat, in his *Quaint Treatise*, looks as effective as ever a hundred years later, whereas many old fancy flies now seem merely quaint.

The term 'imitation' is, of course, misleading to begin with. It expresses good intentions and reflects angling history, but the best of our materials do not approach the delicacy of a natural mayfly spinner. Even if they did, we would still have the problem of a hook, which distorts our efforts. Our designs must be modified to compensate for the crudeness of our medium. Careful fly-tyers often speak of a 'representation' or 'suggestion' of the natural, rather than 'imitation'. (In this book, I shall use the terms almost interchangeably, which seems the most honest of the alternatives, but I do not think there is any such thing as an *exact* imitation.)

Anglers who think of their flies as representations are more likely to avoid the pitfalls in some patterns, such as the use of precisely three hackle fibres for tails, or the use of fragile, stiff wings. Probably the best approach is to suggest as many as possible of the natural's *prominent* features, even exaggerating some of them, while overlooking minor points.

Reg Righyni

By Night for Sea Trout?

'Never disturb the pool until the last light of day has gone!' That is often repeated, and by so many sea trout fishers is believed to be sound policy that to disobey it feels almost to be poaching. Yet the failing light and dusk often offer the best and sometimes only opportunity of sport with these exciting fish.

The approach to the problem requiring that the angler should be denied this delightful spell is perhaps not very penal as far as seasoned night fishers are concerned. It is not every angler, however, who can settle down happily to fish in the dark. Considerable numbers abandon all efforts to get used to night fishing because they regretfully discover that they simply cannot concentrate when they are not able to see in detail what they are doing. For them, discouragement about fishing around dusk is obviously to be deplored and therefore, for their sake and that of novices, a re-examination of the habits of sea trout, with emphasis on that particular question, is much overdue.

Without any risk of robbing the sea trout of his somewhat mystic charm, it can be said that his life as an adult fish in fresh water is not at all difficult to understand – he is, in fact, an uncomplicated fish. He has a big appetite, is an aggressive feeder, and is extremely fond of flies. It so happens, though, that in the normally warm weather of the period when the sea trout begin to arrive in big numbers, there is not much regular, worthwhile fly life on the water during the daytime, then the fish rest in the security of the deep pools, preferably under trees. Apart from being tempted by the occasional dun, spinner or titbit that drops from the leaves, they lie quietly waiting for the great feast that they can expect when the light begins to fade.

It is well to remember here that any good seat trout river when fully stocked has to carry a far greater head of fish than could be supported if they were brown trout and had to be accommodated throughout the year. Consequently the fish are usually found to be in dense concentrations in the more desirable places. And whether or not they have the instinct to shoal, they have no choice than to behave as if that were their inclination.

Even from late evening onwards, when sea trout are well distributed over all the best feeding areas, they are necessarily comparatively close together. Consequently, they get the benefit of the shoal system of warning. But the alarms are not remembered indefinitely as some would have us to believe. When the feast starts, often well in advance of the night proper, the distress of a hooked fish causes a minimum of upset amongst others and sea trout frequently are brought to the net in quick succession.

Admittedly when the expected fare is not forthcoming, a serious disturbance will make them vacate their prospective feeding stations. But this applies during the night as well as at dusk, and in any case – even when there is no reason for the sea trout to be scared – they do not remain indefinitely in any one place if their search for food there is unsuccessful. Furthermore, whatever the cause of their departure, they return rapidly to the advantageous positions where there are flies to be had.

Nevertheless, it must be recognised that anglers who solemnly adhere to the principle that operations should never commence until nightfall, presumably consider that the controlling characteristic of the sea trout is extreme shyness – especially in the daytime – and that once their suspicions have been aroused it takes a long time for them to settle down again into a responsive mood. These people seem to get the idea chiefly from the fact that certain methods employing large, slow-moving lures are not – in a clear water – effective until dark, but that cannot be accepted as the proof of shyness that it is assumed to be. It is far more likely that the failure of the big artificials before dark is because the fish do not associate them with the then ruling conditions and do not see natural creatures of similar size and behaviour until night-time. That explanation would seem to be confirmed by the frequent ready response of the sea trout towards dusk to smaller artificials more in keeping with natural flies which they expect to see at that time, even though the latter are not currently in evidence. Furthermore, reasonably cautious fishing with suitable flies before the arrival of darkness does not put the fish down, either immediately or subsequently, and most anglers are well able to demonstrate that if they try.

Thus the interpretation of the ordinary available evidence can only reasonably be that the food situation is the decidedly dominant influence in the habits of the sea trout, and not an undue tendency to shyness. Strategy can therefore safely be based on the simple fact that if the fly food is available, the sea trout will be in the best feeding positions and ready to respond providing that just ordinary precautions are observed. If there are no flies excepting around dusk no amount of skill makes very much difference and the catches will not be heavy.

It is chiefly a matter, then, of trying to judge if and when there will be a suitable number of flies. Everybody is familiar with the warm, humid conditions that are the most favourable and in that respect there are no difficulties. Unfortunately, however, the change from day to night is subject to being accompanied by a very marked and sudden change in the state of the atmosphere. Frequently a late evening that looks most promising is followed by a rapidly clearing sky and quick drop in temperature. Conversely, very indifferent weather before dark can develop into more or less what is wanted when the night begins.

The common belief that most creatures of nature are instinctively aware of coming changes in the weather does not seem to hold good in respect of the sea trout's ability correctly to foresee the non-arrival of the much wanted flies. Almost without fail and regardless of the weather, they are alerted by the change of light as dusk approaches. Then, as previously indicated, all the good casts will usually yield fish for at least a short spell, irrespective of the presence or otherwise of natural flies.

If the flies do not materialise, the river eventually goes dead and fishing is pretty useless, but that applies whether or not the feeding fish have been covered by the angler during dusk. When a plentiful supply of flies does appear, the brisk sport of dusk continues well into the night with, perhaps, occasional gaps that coincide with the spells when for some reason or other the flies become temporarily scarce.

Should all activity stop with the arrival of darkness however, the angler who has started soon enough might well already be generously rewarded for his visit to the river. And such a sea trout fisher will no longer heed the warnings that the shyness of the fish dictates the sacrifice of that invaluable period of sport around dusk.

The newcomer to sea trout will probably find it very difficult to avoid involvement in the acute partisanship which persists on most rivers concerning the method of presenting the fly. If his own preferences and judgment are to have much chance, he must first appreciate one extraordinary aspect of the sport.

It is this: the really dashing furious fighting ability of the sea trout, that has had such a thrilling appeal to all generations of fly-fishers, is much more a feature of the medium-sized and smaller ones than of the big specimens.

The latter, nevertheless, tend to steal all the glamour. But they – upwards of 6 pounds – are usually relatively very old fish and they both behave and taste like it too! Their comparatively sluggish, bottom-hugging opposition to the rod is such, nevertheless, that if it happens to be the angler's first introduction to the sport with sea-trout – either personally or as a witness – he will probably think it practically impossible for anything to be better. Then he is in danger of concentrating too much on the deeply sunk, large flies that are favoured by the big-specimen addicts.

If the angler with all-round experience deliberately chooses that method, there is no need for comment. The desire of everyone to have some big sea trout in his personal record must be sympathetically acknowledged. But the newcomer should certainly at least give a trial to fishing near and on the surface with the smaller flies before deciding to settle down permanently to the single-minded quest to beat his previous best fish.

A good night with the big sea trout undoubtedly does much for the ego; that is not thought by all, though, to be enough compensation for the loss of hectic sport available with the smaller fish. Indeed, the way in which 2- or 3-pounders often strip off all the line and a lot of backing in an amazing display of speed and strength – punctuated by fantastic leaps – is considered by many widely experienced anglers, including some big-game fishers, to be the finest sport that is to be had with any fish in the world.

Additionally it is well to remember that the big fish can be very moody and dour, even when everything seems to be favourable. Against that, the smaller sea trout can be relied upon to respond readily whenever the circumstances give them the slightest encouragement. The big fish may be dominant in the record book, but in the memory it is more often the smaller fish that are supreme!

Another consideration which should also be recognised is that there are usually worthwhile numbers of grilse and small summer salmon around when sea trout fishing is in full swing. The larger fly near the bottom is most unlikely ever to interest these other fish, but it is not at all uncommon at both sides of dusk for them to take the popular standard sea trout patterns close to the surface.

For a good mixed bag, however, small salmon flies provide the best all-round prospects. In the late evening, when the fish leave the deeper water in favour of the fast run towards the head of a pool, a Blue Charm on a number 6 low-water iron takes a lot of beating, even a good brown trout will then have a go at it too. In the smoother glides, or where the current becomes steadier and it is necessary to coil some line to help the fly to fish properly, the low-water iron will probably be too light. The patent type of 'short-point double' – say a number 8 – is ideal and a Black Doctor is a very suitable dressing. What is more, the big sea trout do not ignore these small salmon flies. But it is not at all uncommon to be recorded – quite innocently – as salmon, and they might well be quite a lot bigger than the grilse and small summer fish that are taken.

Dry-fly fishing, though, has some inherent valuable advantages when sea trout are the sole objective. For most anglers the visual interest is an extra fascinating feature. This is perhaps at its greatest premium before dark, when a medium sedge is justifiably the most popular fly. But even on quite dark nights it is surprising how the disturbance on the surface, when the fish takes, causes either a break or an increase in the reflection, which can easily be detected. And even when nothing can be seen at all, the exciting smack of the take can be heard, and gives warning to strike. In such conditions a well-greased Black Zulu seems to be more attractive than the bustard-type patterns. If it is fished right into the side at about the speed of the natural Great Red Sedge, the sea trout will often swirl within a foot or two of the angler as they turn rapidly in their manoeuvres to head off the fly, and then take it just before it would, otherwise, be lifted from the water.

From the physical point of view, the dry fly is easier to control effectively, and is much more trouble-free than a team of wet flies. But perhaps the most important thing about the floating artificial –

which is shared to a lesser degree by the heavy fly fished just beneath the surface – is that it can be worked with very good prospects of success over slack areas that often hold a lot of fish, and which are practically useless for the more practised methods.

In most fly-fishing for species other than sea trout, it is usually an obvious matter to decide which will probably be the best way to take full advantage of the particular circumstances. Failing that, there will be little doubt as to the two alternatives that might have equally good claims for a trial, and one of which will probably be the correct answer. The position in regard to sea trout can be much the same as far as the individual is concerned, but it is unlikely that there will ever be agreement among several anglers. The interesting controversy starts up again, and if the prejudices can be subdued sufficiently, the exchange of ideas can often be most profitable.

All methods of fishing are undoubtedly the development of what started out originally as individual styles. In sea trout fishing this process is still very much alive today and there are good chances for any angler to make exciting new discoveries if he refuses to be hidebound by old, unimaginative ideas.

Anton Rodgers

Big Jim

About twenty years ago I was invited to Canada to appear in *The Threepenny Opera* at the trans-Atlantic Stratford. Imagine my delight when, having made enquiries, I discovered that there was a 7-acre lake full of massive brown and rainbow trout within an hour's ride of the theatre. Not only that, I could fish it any time I liked as the owner was the secretary to the theatre's Director of Productions.

As I take my rods wherever I go, I was there like a flash and would spend the whole day, blissfully happy, pulling enormous trout out of this lake. The trouble was, I got so relaxed I found it almost impossible to perform at night, so I had of necessity to ration myself.

During the last week of my stay there, I rang up the owner to thank her for the enormous amount of pleasure the fishing had brought me.

'When are you going back home?' she asked.

'Sunday afternoon,' I replied.

'Oh, well,' she said, 'then you can come out, have Sunday lunch and do a bit of fishing.'

I thought it would be cutting things a little fine as the lake was out in the country, but the offer was too tempting to resist.

Arriving at the lake, I found to my dismay that not only was the lady of the house there but also her two small grandchildren and a very large St Bernard dog, and all of them wished to dance attendance on me while I was trying quietly to fish.

After lunch I thought I would have just one last cast before I packed up my rod and went on my weary way to the airport. I was fishing when suddenly one of the children came rushing up to me shouting: 'Anton, Anton, there's an enormous fish in the boathouse.'

'Really,' I said, 'then we had better go and have a look at it.'

I duly crept along and, sure enough, there was a magnificent trout of at least 10 pounds. My mouth went dry and I thought what a wonderful end to a blissful engagement. Working out the strategy, I told the children what we must do. First I would climb the stairs and go onto the boathouse roof and, when I told them to make a lot of noise, the trout would be frightened and come out into clear water, where I would then cast to it. This was done and the huge fish came out in the bright sunlight, gliding like a menacing U-boat. Immediately I cast to it, dropping the fly about 6 inches in front of its nose. It looked at the fly disdainfully and carried on. I was appalled! Retracting my line I cast again and the fly dropped 3 inches in front of the trout. I swear it looked at the fly and raised its eyebrows, and I could almost hear it say, 'You must be joking!' as it went on its merry way.

By now the children were apoplectic with anticipation, as was I. We had been joined by the St Bernard, who sensed that something was about to happen. Frantically, I cast yet again and, to this day, I believe the trout looked at the fly as if to say, 'Oh, well, I suppose I may as well take it as it's your last day.' And very slowly it sucked the fly into its mouth. With great excitement, I tightened my line and, to my astonishment, I was offered absolutely no resistance. The fish almost turned over on its back and said, 'Take me, do!' I could not believe it.

By now, the children were yelling frantically, the dog was barking, and I was attempting to come down the stairs with rod held high and this magnificent fish at the end of the line. As soon as the dog saw the fish it made a beeline for it, soaking me in the process. Needless to say, I was not going to be cheated of my prey and, after manouevring it out of reach of the dog, I managed to get a hand under it and lift it out. I was about to strike the final blow when I was suddenly attacked by a pang of conscience. Why should I destroy this lovely creature when I was about to fly home to England? No, I would just show it to our hostess and then put it back. So, with the fish held high out of reach of the dog and the children, I walked triumphantly back to the house where my hostess was sitting on the porch.

'There,' I said modestly, 'I had a bit of luck with that one; what do you think?'

'Oh, he is lovely. Where did you get him?'

'In the boathouse.'

'Oh, that's Jim, Grandpa's friend. Grandpa feeds him when he goes fishing. They have grown old together!'

At that moment I thanked God I had not struck the fatal blow, which would not only have killed the fish but would have inevitably destroyed my friendship with my hostess for ever. I know I was let off the hook then and now find I think twice before I kill any fish.

Frances Shand Kydd

When Midnight Strikes Twelve and a Half

Fly-fishing is for me the supreme pastime. Complete enjoyment. I have always fished in Scotland, my favourite river the mighty Spey where my long legs are put to good use in the prodigious wading needed there.

I like to fish alone, choose my own fly and tie it on safely, for my moment of greatest excitement comes with the hooking of the fish. That even exceeds the joy of landing it successfully. Fishing before breakfast – into the river by half past six – and again as darkness falls, these are my favourite times.

I was once fishing the bottom pool of a Spey beat alone, in the dark. The wading was difficult, involving the crossing of a shallow but fast-running current to a deep but gravel-bottomed spit with deeper water and overhanging trees either side. The first objective was to get comfortably organised on the spit, then fish gently down to a tree that marked the end of safety and the beginning of a deep hole.

By the time I reached the tree it was almost totally dark. I thought, rightly, that to be there alone was not prudent. Then, like many fishers, I decided on one last cast! It is a sort of personal challenge, I think, to end the fishing of a pool with a good, long, well-positioned cast. As I made it I remember thinking, 'Please, God, don't send me a fish. I'm in enough trouble as it is!'

Well, I hooked one! My first thought was how to get rid of it. Of course it was way below me and the only way I could move was backwards. So, still hoping to be free of the fish, I decided to play it just where I was. After about fifteen minutes I had the mounting sense that maybe I could land it. But where? As both the fish and I were tiring, I turned, rod over my shoulder, wading stick at the ready, and started the long trek back up the spit against the current. There were frequent pit stops as the fish took further runs.

I was hoping for a salmon on its side by the time I hit the heavy, shallow water and, happily, this happened. By now I was resolute in my determination to land my catch and this I did in a rather clumsy and disorganised way, pushing it up the bank with me squatting behind it. But the method worked.

By now it had turned midnight and I had played the fish for an hour. It weighed exactly 12½ pounds and was fresh from the sea, being covered in sea-lice.

That beautiful salmon taught me, I think, two lessons: First, that it is not very wise to wade alone in the dark; and secondly, that the 'one last cast' to the tail of the pool often does work, even on the most inconvenient of occasions.

Sir Geoffrey Johnson Smith
A Lesson in Self-Sacrifice

A friend of mine was fishing from a rock close to a particularly perilous gorge of rushing water. After three blank days he was desperate. Finally, he hooked a large salmon. After a frantic struggle, just as he managed to beach the fish, he slipped on the rock and fell into the raging waters below.

To his anxious colleagues he cried, 'Don't save me, save the salmon!' They did their best . . .

Sir David Steel

The Wrong Boots?

I t is little wonder that away from my working life I seek the peace and relaxation of fishing, mostly in the Border country near my home. As I walk, rod in hand by lochs and streams, I know I tread the footsteps of James Hogg (the Ettrick Shepherd) and his friend and mentor Sir Walter Scott. So relaxed do I become that my mind strays from *The Lady of the Lake* to that great matriarchal trout at Bowhill in Selkirk. Then I ponder over Scott's 1826 letters to the *Edinburgh Weekly Journal* entitled 'Thoughts on the Proposed Change of Currency'. Then I fish a little more.

It was on the lower Ettrick where, quite by accident, a salmon taught me a lesson in diplomacy. It was the only salmon I had hooked there, a doughty fighter which tired both himself and me just below a road bridge. I was alone during the battle but as I began to reel in the fish I heard a motorcycle stop and the rider came down the sloping bank with an offer of help with the net. In came the fish and out went the net. Too high! The collision knocked the fish off the hook and I watched him flick his tail in a grateful farewell.

I looked at my 'helper' and recognised one of my constituents. My teeth gritted and I thought of the fish; had he kept his mouth closed he would have saved himself quite a lot of trouble. And, with teeth still clenched together, I smiled.

Another lesson came during a visit to Japan when my hosts organised a seafishing trip. The Japanese are very fond of their fishing and are prepared to go to great lengths to ensure their own and their guests' complete enjoyment.

The launch was truly luxurious and large enough to boast a crew of eight, a well-stocked bar, and hi-tech radar, sonar and other fish-finding equipment sufficient to locate a sardine under a polar ice-cap, or so it seemed. While trying to take in all this hi-tech I noticed that, for some reason unknown to me, the whole fishing party including the boat's crew were being kitted out with bright white wellington boots. And so we fished!

At the end of the day we all gathered, still in our bright white wellington boots and surrounded by an emperor's ransom in electronic fish-finding equipment, to admire the total catch. One day's hi-tech fishing had produced a single 3-inch tiddler. It lay there on a gleaming silver plate, its eyes downcast, staring hard at our bright white wellington boots. There may have been just a hint of a sneer on its face.

Dave Whitlock

How Trout Feed

I t is well documented that all salmonids are put off by human or organic chemical odours that are foreign to their environment. A new fly reeking of head cement, Pliobond, varnish, paint, detergent or dyes, as well as human hand scents, might well cause trout to sneeze or cough or look elsewhere for a good mouthful. I'm sure the smell of mink, snake or heron has an equally traumatic effect on a wild trout.

The fly-tyer and fly-fisher should give careful consideration to how his flies smell to a trout. Limiting offensive odours, washing flies carefully, masking such odours, or adding natural food odours will help you achieve optimum results. For example, when I fish subsurface imitations of aquatic food forms, I'll rub the fly with the bottom of a rock or a piece of vegetation taken from the stream. This not only helps eliminate offensive odours, but it also wets the fly to help it sink. There is no doubt that a fly so treated performs better than one that carries human or chemical scents.

A trout can taste and feel sensitively with its mouth as it strikes, inhales, and closes its mouth down on its food. I've often watched a trout mouth and expel an artificial fly unemcumbered by leader or drag. I tossed the fly in the water to study the trout's reaction to its taste and feel. Hard flies, and those made of plastic or enamelled materials, are ejected immediately. Flies constructed of soft materials, especially natural furs, feathers, or soft synthetics, are retained longer or sometimes swallowed. The texture of a natural food or artificial is critical in the flash of time the trout retains the captured food; this is especially true for the underwater, slow-fishing techniques such as nymphing.

As trout grow and mature they become greater masters of their physical abilities and senses, at least until old age overtakes them (usually between seven and nine years). From their earliest days, most trout prefer to collect or intercept their foods. If the supply of aquatic insects or other small, slow-swimming natural aquatic food is plentiful, they will continue to feed largely on them throughout their lives. However, these smaller foods generally become less practical for large adult fish to gather in adequate quantities. So they commonly turn to larger, more available foods, such as minnows, crayfish, amphibians, and small trout. But these live foods require much more active foraging than do the smaller food forms. Adult trout can swim faster; and they usually develop stronger and more heavily toothed jaws for seizing and killing their prey.

There is usually a practical order of large-food preferences after wild adult trout abandon the insects, scuds, and smaller creatures. This is predicated on food value versus ease of gathering. Such food as leeches, tadpoles, crayfish, sculpin, school minnows, individual free-swimming minnows (chubs, whitefish, shiners, and others), and small trout are preferred in that general order. Bottom or deep-swimming large foods are greatly preferred over shallow-water or shallow-swimming foods, again because they are easier to find, flush, chase, and then kill and eat. The leech, crayfish, and sculpin are all extremely practical big-fish foods as each has little defence against the predator trout and dwells on or near the bottom.

The various species of trout, char, grayling, and salmon exhibit individual characteristics. The differences between wild-born trout, trout stocked as fry, and domesticated hatchery trout can be drastic also. Tame trout live by differently conditioned reflexes and standards than do wild-born or stocked-as-fry fish. Knowledge of this can be of great value to the angler. For instance, brown trout and to a slightly lesser extent brook trout are twilight and night-time feeders. Both commonly 'hole-up' in the daytime under objects, in beds of aquatic vegetation, or on the bottoms of deep pools, pockets, or holes. They often sleep all day and stir only as the sun begins to set. Though this is not always so, it occurs commonly across their range during the warmer months.

Rainbows and cutthroats are classic daytime feeders. They prefer to suspend themselves off the bottom adjacent to cover but not beneath or in it unless danger is present. Often they flee from their enemies rather than hide from them. Even sleeping or resting they suspend off the bottom in relatively open areas and seldom allow any major objects to pass by unnoticed.

Thus it is easier to see why a rainbow would be considered easier to take on a fly than a brown on most days. It is swimming, wide awake, and ready when most of us are on the water. The brown isn't caught because it is deep, asleep, or waiting for darkness to feed. If you fished only at night you might well think browns more gullible or plentiful than the light-loving rainbows present in perhaps equal numbers in the same waters.

A domesticated or manmade 'plastic' hatchery trout of either species is probably motivated to a frenzy of feeding by a man-set clock time and the sound of thousands of pea-sized pellets striking the water. This continues for as long as a year after these trout have been dumped in the water. I've taken a handful of small bits of gravel and cast it over the surface of a pool that contained stocked trout. In seconds, thirty or forty 8- to 10-inch, pellet-begging, grey-spotted forms would appear at the surface around my feet.

Such unusual environmental conditions as tailwater releases, snow runoffs, rains, droughts, storms, and temperature extremes can drastically alter trout feeding cycles. Major hatches or aquatic-food migrations can also throw normal cycles off. An alert fly-fisher quickly recognises these key changes and uses them to his advantage.

With these physical and sensory characteristics in mind let's look at several hypothetical situations and relate how a trout locates and takes its food.

Nymphing. There is a classic mayfly hatch on a clear trout stream. A nice wild rainbow trout is holding in 2 feet of water just below a riffle. It has adjusted its weight so it can suspend about 8 inches off the bottom and is eagerly intercepting the rising nymphs. A weighted, soft-fur nymph is cast about 15 feet above the working trout and sinks about a foot before it drifts more or less straight downstream toward the waiting trout. The noise level of the dancing riffle masks its splashdown entry from the rainbow's ears. The trout senses the nymph's movement about 4 feet upstream and to its left with its sensitive peripheral vision. It turns toward the nymph using its dorsal and pelvic fins so it can see the nymph more clearly as it approaches. Interested now, it cocks its pectoral fins up and begins to drift back while rising upward to meet the nymph. As it intercepts the fly it watches, sniffs, and then opens its mouth to inhale the nymph. Once the nymph is captured, the pectoral fin edges bend down and the trout begins a drifting dive back toward the bottom. Now it planes down and leisurely swims back to its holding position as it attempts to swallow the fake nymph.

In this case, the trout principally uses its vision, smell and touch senses and bodily movement to locate and capture the nymph.

A night minnow-feeding brown trout. It is two hours after dark and there is no moon. A large brown trout is cruising around a big pool searching for its nightly prey of sculpins, crayfish, and large surface insects. The fly, a large, dark, deerhair-head sculpin is cast across the tail of the pool. The brown hears the big streamer plop down and it stops, tenses, and becomes silent. Next, the streamer is stripped slowly across the bottom, sometimes swimming, sometimes bouncing off rocks, aquatic vegetation, and sunken tree limbs. The brown detects from these movements the pressure waves and noises. Slowly at first, it begins to swim toward the fly. The closer it gets the more accurately it interprets the fly's distance, size, and speed with its lateral-line sensor. About 2 feet away, the brown sees the fly's outline and surges to it for the kill. The sense of touch is next used as the brown strikes the sculpin with stunning closed-jaw blows. Something is drastically wrong! It does not give off a characteristic panic odour, blood smell, or injured vibrations. It has a horrible unnatural odour. So the brown follows the streamer, smelling its wake for several yards, then turns and swims away seeking another, more realistic prey.

In this case, darkness restricted the trout's distance vision so it used its ears and lateral-line sensor to detect and locate its prey. But its senses of sight and touch and smell were all used in the final decision to strike but not to eat the object.

As you can see in these simple examples, trout use various combinations of their body attributes and senses to find, identify, and take or reject possible food. A consistently productive fly-fisher will understand these things and choose his fly designs and fish them accordingly. Knowledge of a trout's senses, the water's environmental condition, and reading the water are, therefore, the three keys to fishing the right artificial.

With all the keenly honed natural instincts and senses a wild trout possesses, you might feel catching them on imitations is an almost impossible task. Actually, the opposite is true. Wild trout are not difficult to catch on flies if your flies, tackle, and methods are chosen with proper understanding of the situation. Realise your mistakes as you observe a trout's reaction to your attempts to catch them; are they not biting, is it too hot or cold, not there, frightened, selective, or just not interested in your offering for another reason? Fly refusal or acceptance is explainable if you understand the fish. Ignorance of basic facts can handicap you for years, while knowledge of them can and will accelerate your success and pleasure as a fisherman.

Lee Wulff

The Trout's World

We live in a world of predators and prey; Man has been the fiercest predator of all. When we fish for trout, a predatory act in which we seek to capture a living animal, we are allied with the hawks that prey on the pigeons, we are one with the wolves that take the caribou and the lion that stalks the gazelle. We take pride now in being nonpreying predators and releasing our fish; but we cannot release a fish until we have captured it so we are still as much predators as ever whether we keep our fish or put them back. To be a good angler one must be a good predator.

The best fishermen are born to it. The great musicians are born with the gift. So are the great anglers. Intelligent people without the gift can learn the techniques and attain considerable proficiency in either music or angling but they will never be able to go as far as those born with the inherent understanding.

To learn to be a good predator one must study predators whether they be cats or hawks or very successful fishermen. When I watch Ed Van Put, one of the best trout fishermen I know, cast his fly I am reminded of a cat stalking a bird; in him I see the same intentness and singleness of purpose. There is a concentration on his quarry that one does not see in the casual fly fisherman. I know that in his mind there is a picture of the water he fishes over that is not limited to the surface he can see but the flowing liquid beneath it and the imagined trout he is trying to catch as they lie in or move through their life medium. They may or may not be there – but they are likely to be where he has learned they should be and they are likely to respond to the flies he has had them respond to before.

I hope you will develop a similar sense of the flowing waters and the trout's positions in them; I hope you, like Ed, will become one with the real world of nature, the world of predators and prey and the ever-changing balance that is part of their lives.

Man was a hunter for most of his time on earth. It was only 6,000 years ago that he became a farmer, which let him cease to be a nomad and settle into cities since he could then store food instead of having to capture or find it anew for each set of hunger pangs. We have been industrial for less than 200 years, which further expanded our ability or need to live in cities and further divorced us from living in and with and understanding the natural world. And what does this have to do with trout fishing?

Because of our changed situation, we have changed our society to adapt to our agrarian, industrial system. To understand wild things and how they live we must unlearn some of the basic tenets of our human society. Humans say, 'Save the children first.' This is natural for us and beneficial to our society. Nature says the opposite. When there is a cold winter with lots of heavy snow, which are the deer that die first? They are the fawns and the smaller deer that are weaker and cannot browse as high as the big bucks and larger does; and so they die of starvation. Nature's premise is that fawns would not be bearing more young the following spring and that the stronger does will, and that the herd will bounce back faster; nature supports the progeny of the best and strongest breeding stock.

Nature is not sentimental. Most city folk are loathe to accept the fact that every living thing will die and most things die violently, by predation and starvation and not of old age. The wild world is a wonderful world. Man may consider it cruel but it is fair. It is a world of predators and prey. We have learned not to hate hawks because, in nature's plan, they are one of the killers like wolves and lions and leopards. It is as much a part of our heritage as it is that of the grizzly. Man may have originated as a vegetarian, but he became the fiercest predator of all, with the power to control all the other animals and build the civilisations we have now.

One may ask, 'Which is the superior or higher form of life, the hawk or the dove?' This is a question about nature, not about the Vietnam War. And the answer is that the predator is essentially superior to the prey. It must outfly, outrun, or out-think the living prey it feeds on. The balancing fact that nature gives to the prey is love – the prey can breed faster. Predators have a lower birth rate and must spend more time training their young to be swifter than their prey and as deadly as possible.

Arthur Godfrey used to say that Man was the only animal who killed for pleasure. He had never seen a fox in a hen house, I guess, and had the fox kill every hen in it not for food but for fun. He felt animals killed only what they needed. But lions don't eat everything they kill; they leave a great deal for the scavengers that follow them. Predators kill for practice and want to be as good as they can be at the skills that keep them alive. Instinctively they know that some day life will be severe and the best of their breed, the ablest killers, will survive and the less capable will die.

Why do I include this lesson on nature in a trout-fishing book? Lions and foxes are a long way from trout! It is because you should shake yourself free from human thinking if you are going to be able to evaluate the actions of a fish like the trout accurately.

Let us now consider the trout. He is a mid-range predator. Half the time he is scaring minnows and insects to death and the other half he is scared to death by bigger fish, and by fish-hawks, fierce eels, otters, mink,

and the like. Of course, no animal can be scared to death, even half the time, and not go off the deep end. So trout, like other forms of prey, find zones of safety in which they can relax. This is very important to the trout fisherman. A trout, to be catchable, must be relaxed and predatory, not scared. A good trout fisherman should know what scares a trout and makes it uneasy and what circumstances will let it relax and think about food rather than safety.

It may be as well at this point to note the trout's three primary needs: safety, food, and comfort. His first consideration is not to be killed. His second is to get enough food to stay alive and hopefully enough to be happy. A trout also wants to be comfortable – for discomfort is troubling and extreme discomfort, such as water too warm for him to function in, will kill him. A fourth factor, sex, will affect his activities but with fish this is occasional and has to be considered only on spawning runs.

To understand the trout we must first realise that he is relatively low on the scale of intelligence. He is not as bright as your two-year-old or your Labrador. He is low on the order of brain power. That doesn't mean he cannot think. He can. Like the old saying, 'Once bitten, twice shy,' he can learn from experience. But too many people give him credit for knowing what humans know or for thinking like a human. No trout has ever seen a steel mill or knows a hook as a hook unless it has been caught on hooks with their distinctive shape at least a few times. No trout knows that a leader is a leader. He may recognise it as something unnatural attached to what would otherwise seem to be an edible fly – but he does not know very much.

Trout live on their past – like spiders and beavers and weaver birds. Can you spin a spider's web? It would take quite a bit of engineering for a human to create something so delicate and so efficient. Yet a spider with a brain smaller than a bit of dust can do it. If you take a pair of beavers and put them in a closed-in swimming pool and feed them for three generations then turn one of the kits loose the first thing it will do in the wild is build a dam. How much training would it take you to build a dam as efficiently as a beaver with only sticks and mud? Take a pair of weaver birds and keep them in an aviary with only the food they need and send the third generation out into the wild and they will build a nest and use the same special knots their great-grandparents used, never having seen it before or been taught in any manner to make that special knot.

Animals like the trout and the beaver live on the inherited skills of their forebears, which we call instinct. To understand trout you must understand their instinctive reactions. That can be learned through observation. Back in 1947, while flying home from Newfoundland in a Piper Cub, I passed over the tuna fishing grounds off Wedgeport where I'd caught tuna and been a part of that early fishery. I saw the sportfishing boats beneath me, trolling baits. I knew some of the boats and captains and swung low over them to wave although I knew they wouldn't know who was in the plane. Then I saw three big tuna swimming at the surface and circled to have a good look at them. Accidentally, the shadow of my plane crossed them and with a great splash of white water they disappeared in the depths.

No bird is big enough to pick up a 1¼-ton tuna and fly away with it yet those fish were scared to death. Maybe when they were tiny a diving bird could have eaten them; but they'd grown to a size where they need have a fear of birds no longer. Still, the fear of something flying was still with them as strongly as ever. Instincts like that are a part of survival. The fish with such instincts have a better survival rate than those that do not. Lower animals survive on many such things embedded in their consciousness. These instincts, which sometimes save them, can be used to capture them as well.

Prior to that incident with the tuna I had been exploring Newfoundland's salmon rivers, estimating their fishing potential and writing about the region's great fishing. I would hike in to a remote stream, camp there and fish; I judged by the fish I could catch in a given time and those I saw and the prevalence of young salmon what the river's potential was. After scaring the tuna I simply waited for a sunny day when the river was running clear and would fly up over the pools of an unknown river at about 250 feet and throw the shadow of the plane upon the pool below. Every salmon in the pool would move in fright and I could tell in a minute or two over a pool what had taken me days and miles of hiking before.

Instincts, once established, are slow to fade. In Newfoundland, when I first went down there in the early thirties, there were many harbour seals that swam up into the river to feed on trout and salmon. As a result, I believe, most of the big trout and salmon used to ease in along shore to the shallow water during the night hours in order to make it more difficult for the seals to surprise them. These seals were host to a worm that infested the codfish of that area so a bounty was put on the seals and they were swiftly eliminated from the sea and streams. Yet the big trout and salmon will continue to ease in against the shore at night for centuries just as big tuna will still dive from a shadow moving over the sea. It is worthwhile to learn the unthinking weaknesses and strengths of the trout you fish for.

We are still studying nature and have not yet started to fish. And there is more. Trout fishing was a challenging sport when catching other types of fish was simple. The challenge came because the trout's food was made up largely of aquatic insects, many so small that imitating them was a difficult and intriguing problem. The magic in a trout stream lies partly in the insects within it. Some are able to change from a living, swimming submarine to a living, flying aeroplane in a matter of seconds. Some come to the top of the water and, bursting through the surface, fly away. Some drift on the surface just long enough to shed their wet suits and fly off in their pilot's garb. Some crawl out on stones to break out of their underwater clothing and into flying gear that will let them go where the trout can't get at them. All must come back to the water to lay their eggs, usually just dapping down on the surface for the briefest touch-and-go without giving a hungry trout a fair chance to get them.

These aquatic insects have been identified and catalogued and many studious anglers know the Latin names they go by. But trout do not know these names. They know the bugs and they know which ones they like and that is what a good trout fisherman wants to know. The need to know the Latin names is only for identification when talking to another angler so that each may understand the other. Being an artist I can draw or describe any insect I find on a trout stream and so have been slow to learn the Latin names.

Trout eat living things, not grasses as carp and suckers do. Anything that moves is fair game and the scope of their feeding is as wide as the sky. As a tiny trout starts to feed he takes into his mouth everything that comes along small enough to get into it; and, sometimes, he will take in things he can only swallow if he chews them apart. A fish has no hands and can only examine anything by taking it into his mouth. This is a point to remember: a curious trout will take into his mouth for an instant something he wants to investigate, something he may have only the slightest feeling he'll want to eat or hope will be worth eating.

The growing trout soon learns that most things that drift freely with the current, like bits of wood and leaf and other debris, have no nutritional value; he learns to let them drift on by, saving his energy for what will nourish him. A trout must get enough food to make up for the energy he expends in getting it. But a good predator will have an extra supply of energy for emergencies and to spend, sometimes, out of the pure joy of living or in practice to build strengths and skills against the competition or hard times to come.

Many of us who fish for brook trout have been lucky enough to see one come out of the water in a clean leap and, descending head first, take our fly on his return to the water instead of coming up to get it from below. What we have seen is sheer exuberance, and pride in a skilful manoeuvre. I have seen the same thing with a rare salmon. Why does it happen? Is it showing off because in earlier feeding the fish has gained so much energy for the effort he's put into it that he has energy to spare? Is it to show off for his own satisfaction or for another trout that might be there to see? Fish are keenly aware of other fish. And they are highly competitive. If I get a particularly savage strike at my fly my first thought is that there may be another (or other) trout close by and my trout raced to get there first.

Curiosity and jealousy are both present. How many times have I seen one trout follow another that was hooked until my presence was definitely determined as dangerous? It was probably because the following fish thought the hooked one had a morsel too big to handle and that he, the second fish, might muscle in and get a share. This happens often with bass. A bass hooked on a plug that stays outside the fish's mouth will be followed by another who will strike at the plug to take it away, occasionally being hooked and landed, both fish attached to the same multiple-hooked lure. This competitiveness is true with trout. It is true with bass. It is true with seagulls and with practically all predators.

Feeding trout in our ponds one sees their competition and jealousy.

When I throw out a handful of pellets they rush swiftly to get those they can see before other fish do. However, if I throw pellets in one at a time when they're hungry they'll rush for them at top speed to get there ahead of the other trout. Often they'll bump into each other hard as they make contact at the pellet. On one occasion two trout came at the pellet from opposite directions and the 12 incher's head drove right into the mouth of the 18 incher coming the other way.

The trout learns that the things that move, either through the water or within themselves (like the pulsating of a mayfly's gills or the swimming motion of a nymph's legs or body) are living and edible. Motion becomes his first and major criterion as to whether something he sees is edible and worth chasing or not. Motion, either of or within a fly, has caught more trout than anything else.

To understand this better it is important to realise that for the first four centuries of fly fishing only wet flies were used. Wet flies are built with wings and a body, hackle (legs) and tail. Trout rarely if ever expected to see a winged insect moving under the water and no winged flying insect ever wanted to be there. Yet in those early centuries thousands of trout were caught on wet flies and the early British anglers scoured the world for the fanciest of feathers to make them beautiful. When fly fishermen finally realised that winged flies under water – with few exceptions – were unnatural, they began to shift to imitations of the underwater forms of the aquatic insects, the nymphs; then hundreds and hundreds of the early wet-fly patterns many anglers thought they could not do without drifted off into oblivion.

Even today as many or more trout are caught on flies no trout ever dreamed of seeing than on imitations of the old standbys they feed on. The trout, a tough competitor in his class, sees something drifting along towards him. He's never seen anything like it. But it moves and must be alive. He grabs it before some other trout can get to it. Maybe it is a beetle that rarely or never gets to a stream. It might be a praying mantis, the first insect of its kind ever in that stream's valley, or a Mickey Finn, a streamer fly of red and yellow and silver, that looks like nothing he has ever seen before.

Picture the trout lying in his selected feeding spot. A few hunger pangs heighten his awareness of things around him. He's strong and feisty on this late spring day. Along comes something swimming or drifting across his vision. He's old enough and wise enough to have a little caution, having been hooked and escaped a time or two; but this thing is intriguing. It has colours in a combination never seen before. It swims in a way that's most unusual. He studies it and realises that this is something truly different.

But what is it?

Is it good to eat?

What will it taste like?

It's moving out of range and it's now or never. If he lets it go by he'll never know what it would taste like and he decides to find out. They say curiousity kills cats; the same holds true for trout.

Trout will hide and when they have hidden you cannot catch them on a fly. I have waded across the Beaverkill and, stepping on a flat-topped stone, sent a good trout scurrying out from under it to safer water somewhere else. Trout will ease in under overhanging banks and nestle in hiding against the earth or roots or weed growth. On a caribou-hunting trip our luck was poor at first and, in order to get some trout to vary our diet from bacon and beans, I 'tiggled' some trout. I would walk along the edge of the stream until I saw a fish dart in under the bank. Then, quietly, I would slowly feel around with my hand until I found the trout. A gentle stroking on their flesh seems to soothe rather than to bother them. When the exact position of the fish is determined a quick closing of the hand can provide a grip that will hold them. 'Tiggling' is an old poacher's method that requires no complex tackle, just understanding and skill.

It is easy to see that there is a great deal to learn about the trout and his ways. We have made a beginning. Studying the ways of trout can be a lifelong interest, with new and surprising insights possible for even the wisest of old-time anglers.

Ted Entwhistle

Jam Jar or Crystal Ball?

The fascination with fish and fishing came to me when I was about six years of age. I saw some lads walking away from a local pond with poles slung over their shoulders. They were carrying a big jam jar slopping water and containing small rudd. At least the fish had red fins and were not very big, so I guess that is what they were. I was so entranced by these creatures, twisting and turning in their glass cage, that I followed along, trying to get a better look, until I was asked, "Ere, wot yer after? Clear orf.' I went on about my business a bit miffed, but from then on was smitten. I wanted to catch fish myself.

My father had no interest in fishing whatsoever and never did know one end of a rod from the other, so I got no encouragement from him. I had to go it alone. Initially my fishing was bent pin stuff. My first rod was a length of bamboo, the guides were bent hairgrips fixed with a sticky cloth tape. The reel was a cotton reel with a small nail for a handle. It was attached to the rod by a bigger nail bent over and lashed on with sticky tape and string. About 5 yards of flax line was wound on and a cork made an adequate float. A piece of gut made a trace. Although I used a bent pin a couple of times, my shilling a week pocket money did run to buying a few proper hooks, but all in all my outfit was very crude. It was good enough to catch eels and the occasional trout in the local brook, though.

Shortly after I had managed to get my interest in fishing off the ground, we moved to live by the sea. A school chum, aware of my interest, invited me to go fishing off the local beach. He even offered to supply me with tackle, an offer I accepted gratefully, knowing that my own rudimentary gear would be totally inadequate for fishing in the ocean. Who knew what I might hook?

I duly met up with my friend on the beach at Hordle Cliff in Hampshire on a beautiful spring day. He proceeded to assemble a superb, gleaming rod which he said was made of greenheart, and had been given to him on his birthday. My jaw dropped when I saw the reel: it was an Ocean City multiplier, which I had heard cost £5, the best part of a week's wages for an adult at that time. My pal said he could cast over 70 yards with this outfit. From my limited knowledge at that time, his equipment seemed the best that money could buy.

I could not wait to see what he had for me to use. He handed me a short rod which had been made from a golf-club handle. That brought me down to earth! However, it was fitted with a genuine fishing reel, a Nottingham starback loaded with cuttyhunk line. He demonstrated a sort of sidecast along the beach with this outfit. It went about 20 yards. I had a couple of practice casts myself, then baited up with ragworm and cast out to sea – well, a sort of 15-yard lob really, just beyond the slight surf. My companion also cast his bait, though with his superior tackle a good deal further. In a little while I felt a sharp tug on my line and, on winding in, a plump, silver scaled fish appeared out of the waves, attached to my hook. I was told it was a school bass weighing about 2 pounds and would make excellent eating. I took it home, my mother cooked it, and we had it for supper. It was my first sea fish and now I was really hooked.

At low tide I went back to the beach where the bass had taken my bait. A noticeable gully ran close inshore where my bait had been lying, and beyond was a fairly barren sandbar stretching some 60 or 70 yards offshore. I thought to myself that there was a lesson to be learned from this. That inshore gully looked as if it should be attractive to fish. Moreover, while the ability to distance cast could increase the options, it would be easy to cast over fish and miss an opportunity.

My family took my fishing more seriously after I had caught that first bass and soon afterwards I received a war-surplus tank radio aerial as a birthday present. These aerials could be made into very useful fishing rods. They came in three sections spigotted together, in total about 14 feet long. They were made of copper-coated tubular steel and over the next few years, while they were still available, I made several up into rods. The top 5 or 6 feet, when fitted with a few rod rings and a cork handle, made up into a handy light rod, ideal for the local stream. The lower section of 8 or 9 feet made a useful beach and pier rod capable, with my well oiled starback reel, monofilament line, and 5-ounce lead, of casting some 60 yards when necessary.

I was enthralled with fishing and soon I would be off every Saturday night, weather permitting with some of my chums to fish off the shore at Hurst Castle. Initially we walked the shingle spit to get to the old fort. Later we regularly obtained a rowing boat from Cap'n Adams' boatyard at Keyhaven. I recall that around this time we encouraged one of our school friends, who had never fished before, to join us one Saturday night. He agreed and the next Saturday, having kitted him out, we rowed off down the Keyhaven river in the *Lally*, a 12-foot dinghy, one of Cap'n Adams' finest, and my favourite.

Arriving at Hurst Castle, we pulled the dinghy up the inner, sheltered beach, crossed the spit, and set up our rods on the edge of the sandbar known to yachtsmen as The Trap. This sandbar faces Fort Albert on the Isle of Wight. It was, and still is, a productive bass mark, and the regulars among us all had an ambition to catch a bass of at least 5 pounds. Within an hour of starting to fish our school mate, on his first fishing trip, had hooked and landed a 7-pound bass! The rest of us were green with envy. We caught only school bass and pout that night. We thought we must have a new recruit to the ranks of angling, but when asked if he was coming on our next foray he declined. 'It's boring!' was his comment. To this day, more than forty years on, his lack of appreciation of that fish still irks me. But it makes the point that angling is a passion and not everyone, even given the opportunity, will enjoy it.

Rowing to Hurst in Cap'n Adams' *Lally* soon led to fishing from the dinghy. My transition to boat angling had begun. I learned a lot about tides, bait gathering, weather, and small-boat handling as I grew up on and around the western Solent. As a young man I joined the Merchant Navy and spent eight years at sea. On all my travels I took a fishing rod. Eventually, when I came ashore, I bought the first of what was to be a succession of small boats for sea angling.

Once I had my own boat, I developed a particular fondness for smooth-hound fishing. I especially enjoyed fishing for them in the sheltered, inshore waters of the Solent – and I still do. For me, there is something particularly tranquil about being on the water on a warm summer evening, listening to cattle lowing, hearing a pheasant call or a fox bark, catching the scent of barnyard and woodsmoke aromas drifting off the shore. There is something special above seeing the rod tip twitch in the gathering gloom as the first investigative bump from a hound is transmitted up the rod, and moments later hearing the reel scream as the fish runs with the bait. Then a grey torpedo shape appears near the surface in the headlamp's glow. Finally, there is the satisfaction as the fish, released, surges away with a flick of its tail.

My boating has moved on. My latest craft is fitted with all the modern technical aids. They allow me to roam the English Channel, weather permitting, more or less at will. I can take the shortest route to a wreck, set up a guard zone on the radar, see my current location on a chart plotter, speak to my wife on the mobile phone, and have shipping forecasts automatically recorded.

Today, when I can afford it, I like nothing better than visiting exotic locations in pursuit of saltwater game fish – fish such as marlin, tuna, sailfish, and makos. On one such trip, fishing a 6-kilogram line in a line class competition, a mako of about 170-pounds grabbed the Rapala I was trolling. It was intended for long fin tuna, but the shark did not know that. For three hours that shark and I tussled. He exploded clear of the water on several occasions, and five times I had the fish to the side of the boat. Twice I had the double line on the reel with the 80-pound leader in the rings. Finally, on the fifth occasion, the fish, now very tired, hung in the tide against the boat's wind drift, his snout angled in toward the bow, the beautiful slate-blue body shining in the water. We were fast running out of time. The skipper suggested a burst from the engines in order to kick the boat's stern round and lay the fish alongside. I agreed, the engines fired, and the fish took off straight under the bow! The short stand-up rod I was using was not long enough when thrust underwater to allow the line to clear the keel. It was 'Goodbye, mako!' and I was left with just another memory of one that had got away.

The future? Who knows? More great fish? A new boat? Probably, and all from a jam jar of little fish that I can still see in my mind's eye.

Peter Lapsley

Mad Dogs and Englishmen

Those of us who fish chiefly in the British Isles are not easily overawed by our quarry. Most coarse fish are reasonably manageable – apart perhaps from the occasional unexpectedly large or maverick barbel, carp or pike. The overstuffed rainbows stocked into some small stillwater fisheries tend, in truth, to fight like sacks full of wet mice. Fit reservoir trout can sometimes produce momentary rushes of adrenalin as they take the line down to the backing. And sea trout may cause pandemonium in a pool for a few minutes before coming quietly to the net. But such dramas are fairly predictable and, generally, we can keep them under control. Even when sea fishing or salmon fishing, we can hazard reasonable guesses as to the size and ferocity of the fish we may encounter and set up our tackle accordingly.

There are places, however, where the variety, size and savageness of the fish make it virtually impossible to plan sensibly, and where one can often become wholly overwhelmed by the sheer enormity and strength of some of the specimens one meets.

Some years ago, as a young Army officer, I spent four sweaty years in the Arabian Gulf. I had been fishing in Britain since boyhood but was still relatively inexperienced, and I was certainly not prepared for the sort of 'sport' I was to find in tropical waters.

A small group of us used to spend a week at a time marooned on Yas Island, just off the coast of Abu Dhabi, practising directing fighter aircraft on to ground targets. It was an ideal place for the purpose – scorched, bleak, barren and uninhabited, a 5 mile by 3 mile lump of sand and rock poking up out of the sea. We camped at the southern end and directed the aircraft's shells and rockets onto targets at the northern end. When the pilots had returned to their home comforts in Bahrain at the end of the day's flying, we made ourselves supper and then whiled away the hours spinning for garfish from the sand bar which enclosed a small lagoon.

Late one evening, and for no particular reason, I sliced a garfish in half, baited up a largish hook with it, put on a small Arlesey bomb and hurled the whole caboodle 75 yards out into the sea, well beyond the steep dropoff we had discovered just offshore. It seemed to go on sinking for ever. When eventually it came to rest, I released the bale-arm on the fixed-spool reel, propped the 7-foot spinning rod against my rucksack and sat down on the sand, chatting with my companions.

Nothing happened for a while and then, quite suddenly, the rod lurched off its support and bounced off down the beach, heading for the water. I grabbed it and struck against what felt like a rock on the bottom. Whatever it was fought not at all, but instead allowed itself simply to be winched, very slowly and gradually, up the side of the sand bar. At last, after what seemed like interminable heaving, hauling, huffing and puffing, we dragged it into the shallows and stranded it on the beach.

When we shone our torches on it, all three of us found ourselves, for the first time in our lives, seriously frightened of a fish. It was huge and hideous, 4½ feet long with a tapered, blubbery black body, a squashed head covered in carbuncles, tiny, malevolent eyes and an array of fangs the like of which I had never seen before and never wish to see again. It did not thrash about. It simply lay there, glaring at us, challenging us to touch it, which we went to considerable lengths to avoid doing. Instead, we cut the wire trace warily, 6 inches or so from the monster's cavernous mouth, and nudged it back towards the depths with the help of a long pole.

I never discovered what this dreadful creature was. Some people say they believe it must have been a species of grouper, although no other groupers I have seen have been so appallingly ugly. Whatever its parentage, it was the sort of apparition that could persuade one to give up fishing for ever – well, almost.

The following year found me serving with the local Arab militia, the Trucial Oman Scouts, near Sharjah, living in a cottage on the beach. I struck up a friendship with a German engineer who was supervising the building of a deep-water jetty for the ruler. Largely complete, it struck out to sea at a 45° angle to the shore. We used to sit on it in the evenings, chatting, enjoying the balmy tropical night air and the odd beer, and fishing in a desultory sort of way, chiefly for garfish and small barracuda, which shoaled in the calm water inside the jetty.

We had caught a few garfish one April evening when a monstrous spectre sidled into the yellowish light cast by the arc-lights – a gigantic shark, 14–16 feet long, swimming lazily and sinuously shorewards immediately below us. Realising that it was heading into a bottleneck and would have to turn round and return along the same route, I jokingly told Fritz that I was going to catch it.

Quickly I fastened the biggest iron I had to a short, braided wire leader, sliced a garfish in half, impaled the tail end on the hook, lifted the bale-arm – and waited. Bear in mind that, foolish youth that I was, I was using a 7-foot spinning rod and an inexpensive fixed-spool reel loaded with about 100 metres of 20-pound monofilament.

Sure enough, the shark came back. As it approached, I dropped the bait about 10 feet in front of it. I am sure I heard it say 'Thank you' as it rolled slightly and ingested the sawn-off piece of fish. I released the bale-arm and raised the rod until it curved over into a hoop. The shark swam on steadily, completely unperturbed, without the slightest change of speed or direction. The reel whined as the line was stripped from it. The

shark disappeared into the darkness. I do not believe it even realised it had been hooked. When it had taken all the line from the reel, the rod-tip pulled inexorably downwards until it was pointing straight out to sea. There was a 'Ping!' as the line broke, and that was that.

A year later, I was posted to Al Hamra, a small camp over 100 miles from the nearest town, near the border between Qatar and Abu Dhabi. There was a pumping station at Jebel Dhana, 20 miles away, where oil was loaded into the cavernous holds of the waiting tankers. From here I went out fishing occasionally on the launch that provisioned these great ships. We caught king mackerel up to 30 pounds but had to move the boat frequently, whenever sharks announced their presence by attacking fish as we reeled them in, chomping them off neatly behind the gill covers.

More often I went off on my own to a low, rocky promontory which jutted out a ½ mile into the sea. Here I whiled away afternoons too hot for work, spinning for garfish in temperatures of up to 115°F.

On one such afternoon, I was sitting on a boulder, gazing out to sea, minding my own business, when a monstrous ray, creamy white underneath, black on top, exploded from the water 100 yards away and 45° to my right, soared through the air, its wing tips curved elegantly upwards, its long, slender tail just fizzing through the water's surface, and splashed back in again 45° to my left. Simple geometry suggests that it must have flown for some 200 yards; I do not doubt it. At a conservative estimate, I reckoned its wing-span to be about 20 feet. It was the most extraordinary sight I have ever seen, by far. I sat mesmerised, staring at the point at which it had disappeared, longing desperately for an encore which never came. Eventually, after perhaps an hour, and with a strange but very strong sense of sadness and anticlimax, I packed up my tackle and headed homeward.

If nothing else, these fish – the 'grouper', the shark and the ray – gave me lessons in humility which will live with me for the rest of my life.

Lord (Roy) Mason of Barnsley

Good Lord, Not Another One!

Having been born in the tiny mining village of Royston, near Barnsley, in 1924, I did what most of my pals did and went to work in the local coal mine. I toiled underground for fourteen years before entering politics and becoming a Member of Parliament. Even in those early mining days I had been bitten by the fishing bug and I well remember those far-off times when I fished off the Yorkshire coast to catch some fresh fish for the table.

Rising at five o'clock on a Sunday morning, I took the coach at six and reached Bridlington or Scarborough at around eight. I sailed on the tide with a bunch of chaps that included miners, publicans, teachers and factory workers. We were after cod, mackerel, whiting, ling and haddock, and I still reserve a few Sundays for these breathtaking sea trips.

Back in the old days, the boat skippers used little high-tech equipment to locate fish-holding spots such as wrecks and 'rough ground', relying mainly on compass readings and lining up with headlands and other features. These days, of course, the use of Decca equipment and other electronic gadgets allows the boats to be positioned over any one of the hundreds of World War Two wrecks.

One thing could be relied on in those years gone by: if the boxes were full of cod and ling etc. at the end of the session on the North Sea, the skipper had got it exactly right. But if we struggled, it was never his fault!

Fish location has come a long way, but tactics for the big fish have remained more or less unchanged. Only the name is different; for 'jigging' read 'pirking'. The idea is to use a boat rod rated 30–50 pounds and a big Scarborough-type centre-pin reel or a multiplier loaded with strong nylon line. On the business end is tied a metal 'pirk', simply a short piece of shiny tubular metal with a hook fastened to it. Many of the lads in the old days used short lengths of cycle handlebar tubes, and (at risk of life and limb) filled them with molten lead.

In attempting this lead-filling method, one local banker in Barnsley wished he had not bothered. There must have been some water or a bit of dampness in the flattened end of the tube; whatever it was, his neighbours thought there had been another explosion at the local pit! The big bang did not kill him, but his wife tried to. Her kitchen was an absolute mess, the gas cooker was covered in lead, her favourite ornament was broken, the goldfish was on the floor, and the cat nearly

had to be shaved to get the lead off it. He soon gave up that idea.

However difficult it was to make these metal lures with lead inside, they worked a treat for those North Sea cod and ling. We lowered them to near the sea bed and started jigging them up and down to attract the quarry. To attract the big fish further, we added coloured pieces of plastic (now called 'muppets') to the ends of the hooks.

We still use the same methods to this very day, the only difference being that it is now often necessary to travel 20 or 30 miles from places such as Whitby to have a good chance of a big catch. But even though fish stocks around Britain have been depleted, there are still times when the rods bend all day. In fact, going back just a few years, a party of ten anglers caught so many cod and ling that they could not get all of them home. Their cars and a trailer were full to the brim with bags of fish, and they ended up giving a lot of it away in Whitby.

In the early days, the anglers were spread far and wide around Barnsley, and the driver of the old twenty-eight- or thirty-two-seater coaches did a lot of picking up in the nearby villages. But despite having to do a few extra miles, we were always on the boat on time. On one dark wintry morning, however, it all nearly went wrong – all because stuttering old Albert from Cudworth, on the main route to Whitby, had moved house during the preceding week.

Number 34 was the message that had come through during the past few days, and, with the help of street lights, we finally found it – with not a sign of life. 'Give door a bang,' shouted Fred. That did not work, so they rattled the windows, and there was still no sign of Albert and not even of his grumpy wife.

By this time, one or two neighbours had got up to see what was going on that Sunday morning, and one or two of the lads on the coach were getting very impatient. In a last attempt to get Albert out of his warm bed, one of our fishermen shouted through the letterbox: 'Get yourself out of bed and onto this bus,' at the same time implying that Albert had never known who his father was.

Then all suddenly went quiet. The door had swung open and standing there looking very angry was a bloke about the size of Frank Bruno with a metal poker in his hand! Obviously we had got the wrong house and, as we raced out of the village, one little man at the back of the coach admitted, 'Oh, dear, I've got the number of the house written on this screwed-up bit of paper – and we should have gone to number 43, not 34!' After that episode, Albert had to meet us at the end of the road, and I bet they are still talking about it at number 34.

I know there are one or two pike anglers who still talk about my first excursions into coarse fishing for, with three rods set up, I found I had hooked three pike at the same time, and one of them just passed the 20-pound mark! Then I tried my hand at shark fishing out of Kinsale and Looe and managed an arm-aching specimen of 100 pounds which encouraged me to go game fishing off the Seychelles, where I had a two-hour battle with a magnificent sailfish which weighed in at 102 pounds and measured 7½ ft from snout to tail. That was an absolutely thrilling and exhausting experience, just like hanging on the edge of a precipice, arms and muscles aching.

Later, off Mauritius, I caught a 44-pound dorado, beating the island record by 2 pounds. Then, while Secretary of State for Northern Ireland, I went out on Strangford Lough and hauled in a specimen tope of 50 pounds.

Now I fish mostly for stillwater trout. My interest started when my local party presented me with some fly tackle to mark my twenty-fifth anniversary as Barnsley's Member of Parliament. Fly fishing for trout has given me a new lease of life since I came out of government. Being Defence Secretary and Northern Ireland Secretary meant I was wearied, worn and constantly on the alert, in a job that demanded attention night and day, so casting to trout has been a sheer joy for me.

Having been able to give something back to the sport that I have loved since I was a lad has also been a joy. Forever making sure that anglers' views are heard at Westminster and in other places, I was a member of a committee established to advise the Government on the best ways to set up the National Rivers Authority. Then, still making sure that anglers got a fair deal, I served as a full board member of the NRA for a full term of two years.

Back in 1987 I started the ball rolling to get rid of separate rod licences for the various areas up and down the country. Like many anglers, I had to buy six or seven different licences to fish areas as far apart as Cumbria and the Thames, and the cost mounted up. At that time many of angling's leading men pooh-poohed the idea of one rod licence and I had to be dogged in my campaign to get fishermen a better deal.

Another hobby-horse of mine has been nylon monofilament nets, and I have campaigned to have these fish killers of the sea banned. I also fought strongly for angling to outlaw the use of chrysoidine dye on maggots and other baits. Scientists list this analine-based colouring agent as a cause of cancer, and it should be handled only with protective gloves and while wearing masks etc. And yet hundreds of anglers from places like Leeds, Liverpool and London still get their hands covered in the stuff every week of the season.

It pleases me that I am still in a position to try and bring improvements for angling and I am especially proud to be associated with the rod licence issue and the introduction of one bit of paper to cover the whole of England and Wales. Now when I visit my favourite stillwaters I feel I have earned the joy of catching lots of silvery rainbows, some of them into double figures, and as I reel in each splashing fish, there is the inevitable comment from anglers nearby: 'Good lord, not another one!'

Peter Peck

Icing on the Cake

Many years ago a grand old fellow that I used to fish with maintained that angling was 70 per cent anticipation, 20 per cent expectation and 10 per cent participation. In all my fifty-plus years of sea angling I have never had cause to doubt this statement.

How is it possible to explain the excitement and pleasure that comes from planning your next excursion on or by the water – preparing tackle, checking rods, reels and lines, making sure that you have made enough traces to cover all possibilities, sharpening hooks, collecting together all those items of tackle that you are sure you will need, shocked by the amount you have gathered but must take – just in case. I am not a loner and I get tremendous pleasure in fishing with my companions. No pleasure ever seems the same if you cannot share it.

Sea angling is not a spectator sport if for no other reason than that the greater part of the action is normally far removed from areas of population. I believe that this is one of the attractions. It also means that most people are totally unaware of this wonderful 'other' world of sea anglers, the sights and experiences that we have whilst pursuing our sport – the remoteness of the surf beach, the vastness of the seas, the sky with its ever changing light and colours. Sunset and sunrise viewed from a boat, alone on the sea are sights never to be forgotten, and the clouds with all their different formations are an encyclopedia of the weather for those who can read them. With the boat rising easily, the sea imparting that slight motion that is almost hypnotic, the sun shining and fish being boated at regular intervals, you ask yourself, 'Why don't I do this every day?' Then when the boat is crashing down between huge swells, you are hanging on to anything that does not move and your friends are not moving as they just want to die quietly, you cast a troubled eye in the direction of where you think land is and ask, 'What on earth am I doing here?'

Being on or by the sea is always rewarding; there is always something to see: birds of every size, shape and description. Gulls wheel and dive, always on the look-out for food – woe betide the angler who puts his sandwiches in full view and turns his back. Gannets, the Stukas of the seabird world, scan the waters for any movement, then peel away, wings closed, plummeting into the water to catch their fish. These are the birds to watch for if you are looking for bait fish. Skuas are the acrobats, letting other birds catch the food and then harassing them until they drop it. It does not matter how much the other bird twists and turns, the skua will be behind it. The regal greater black-backed gull soars and glides over the water, not averse to a little bullying himself when it comes to food. You may be lucky enough sometimes to see the huge flocks of birds, generally ducks and geese, as they set off on their migration or return from it, always in perfect formation – a great sight.

Quite often a small bird, a bumble bee or a butterfly will settle on top of the cabin, and homing pigeons are regular visitors. After a short rest they all go happily on their way. All these things and many more are so much a part of the sea angler's world and the more you fish the greater is your awareness of all the bonuses that are yours to enjoy.

How inadequate is the written word when trying to describe this 'other' world. To accurately portray the emotions that are felt, describe the elements that are encountered and evoke the feelings of satisfaction that are experienced is certainly far beyond my capabilities. One thing, however, is certain and that is that it is the presence of the fish that opens up this other world to us.

I have been very fortunate in my fishing life, and have achieved far more than I could ever have hoped for. I have been able to fish in nearly all parts of the world, have caught many big fish, held several world records and have caught the majority of the well-known species.

During one's angling life there are always certain events that are remembered more than others. They are very few and far between, but one such occasion occurred very early in my sea-angling life. It did not involve any big fish, no records were broken and no exotic location was involved, but it was an experience to be savoured.

The year was 1958, the location the south coast resort of Swanage in Dorset. I was there on a family holiday and had rented a small flat that was accessed from a short promenade which was raised about 6 feet above the sea. The sea was about 20 feet from the front door. Living in the East Midlands, I generally had a round trip of 240 miles each Sunday in order to get a boat out of Great Yarmouth, so having the sea 20 feet from my front door was a chance not to be missed. I had come prepared.

Although I had been boat fishing for a number of years my experience of shore fishing had up to this time consisted in using a casting pole from the beaches of Great Yarmouth. I had, however, arrived at Swanage with a new 8-foot split-cane rod with a fixed-spool reel that my wife had bought me – one of the original 'monkey grinders' – and mono line that was in those days like sprung steel – great stuff as long as it was kept tight, otherwise coil after coil sprang from the reel as quickly as the blink of an eye.

At five in the morning I was leaning against the railings watching the tip of my rod; 50 yards out there were three wriggling ragworms attached to a three-hook brass paternoster. The shopkeeper had assured me they were the thing to do the job. Everything was kept in place on the sea bottom by a large watch lead. I had been fishing for only a short time when a voice behind me asked the question so beloved of anglers. 'Caught anything yet?' I turned to find a middle-aged fellow studying my rod tip with interest. This was the beginning of a great friendship. Ted was from the north and was an ex-miner. He suffered very badly from a lung disease and was at a hotel in Swanage that belonged to the miners' union, to which fellows like him could come for a few days. He was a great conversationalist and quite an authority on racing pigeons. Whenever he talked about them his eyes lit up and he spoke with great enthusiasm.

Over the next few days nothing significant occurred. Occasionally when I reeled in to rebait there would be a small plaice, pouting or more likely a vast number of crabs, all competing for the little shreds of bait that were left. The weather was glorious, perfect late June weather, warm bordering on hot and with a gentle south-westerly breeze. I was centred in Swanage Bay, the sweep round to Ballard Down to my left and Peverill Point to my right – a truly lovely situation with a good friend to keep me company. A number of people stopped to talk and all of them appeared to have a vast knowledge of shore fishing! I was told that it was necessary to have a rag wrapped round the railings and my rod to save the rod from rubbing and stop it being pulled over the side by a fish, a motorboat or large crab. I also learned that it was essential that I have a bell on the top of my rod to indicate the bites. One gentleman even gave me one.

Then on my last day it happened. Suddenly the rod butt left the ground, the bell started ringing, and at five o'clock it sounded very loud. I was rather taken aback, as I had run out of bait and was actually using a strip of bacon rind. I vaguely remembered that at some time I had heard or read that this was an acceptable offering. I frantically started trying to undo the knot in the rag holding the rod to the railings; with the strain of the rod being pulled over it, it had jammed. All this time the rod was jumping about, the bell ringing, and already I could see faces at the windows. One window opened and a loud voice asked what on earth we were doing; the expletives that were interspersed with the words left no doubt that the talker was, to say the least, peeved. I finally succeeded in freeing the rod and lowering the tip, and Ted was able to remove the offending bell; peace prevailed once again. The sea was flat calm, so it was easy to follow the line as it cut through the water, first one way then the other, backwards and forwards. I had set out a reasonably tight drag on the reel and this, coupled with the rather heavy lead, gradually ensured that the runs became shorter and slower. It was now that I saw the fish for the first time. First it was a silver flash then as I worked it close in I could see that it was a bass – my first bass. The next problem was no landing net – I had not anticipated anything like this happening.

Fortunately there was a boat slip at the end of the promenade and Ted told me to work the fish along there and he would do the rest. This I managed to do and the next moment there was Ted knee deep in water clutching this magnificent fish to his chest, somehow managing to avoid the sharp, spiky fins that the bass kept raising. I carefully unhooked if and placed it back in the water, where it lay on its side, its gills opening and closing rapidly, its tail gently moving. What a wonderful sight – my first bass, its silver flanks glistening. I estimated that it weighed about 3 pounds. Ted and I just stood and watched this lovely fish. Everything had been so hectic and now it was all over, our heartbeats returned to normal and the spectators gradually disappeared. There was a sudden movement in the water, a quick twist, a flick of the tail and our fish had gone. The day had returned to normal.

I never saw Ted again, but from that time on I realised that angling is far more than the actual catching of a fish; it requires other factors. On this day the elements were at their very best, the surroundings were idyllic and I had a good companion to share the thrills, excitement, pleasure and satisfaction of a successful day's fishing.

To obtain the maximum pleasure from our sport is like making a good cake. You need all the right ingredients, and catching the fish last is the icing on the cake.

David Profumo

Farewell Banana

I n the wake of my guide, I dropped stealthily over the side of the punt and stood on the porcelain-white substrate of the Pacific sandflat. As the rest of the party chugged off, we began to scan the immediate area for signs of feeding bonefish – it was only the first day of our trip, and my eyes had not yet adjusted to the glare and complicated colours of the equatorial sea, but I could just make out a small shark some way off.

Tyrone and I took a few steps, then he dropped into a crouch. 'Beeg bon,' he hissed, pointing urgently.

I strained to see through the corrugated crystal of the water.

'Where, in relation to that shark?'

'No shark, Dave. Beeg bonfish.'

And now of course I could see that this was indeed a great battleship of a boney, a specimen fish, a real 'Harvey Wallhanger.' The hookpoint snagged in my thumb as I struggled to free it from the keeper ring.

'Man,' said Tyrone. 'Oh, man.'

I would usually contend that any fishing expedition begins the previous night, when knots are made and tackle is stowed. But the stalking of that particular fish really began a whole year earlier, and the process by which our paths finally came to cross was quite elaborate.

There is a Micronesian island some 1,200 miles south of Honolulu, so remote that it makes its own weather, has no TV, and its inhabitants have never heard of OJ (I reckon even our own Queen of Hearts could stroll there incognito). Originally settled by the Polynesians, who followed the migratory path of golden plovers, it was named Christmas by Captain Cook when he landed there on Christmas Eve 1777 to take turtles. There being no 's' in their alphabet, the islanders call it Kiritimati.

For about a year I had been trying to engineer this trip – getting a journalistic commission, cajoling friends into signing up, securing domestic clearance – so this was not exactly a spontaneous away day. As the Air Nauru jet banked for landing, we were peering down onto one of the world's largest coral atolls, a vast volcanic bowl brimming with fish soup. To be honest, it is not a conventionally attractive place: scrub and rock, saltbush and coconut palm, with the highest point just 12 feet above sea level; also, there is a mass of rusting debris shamefully left behind by the British forces (this was a nuclear testing site during the Cold War). But we had not come for the scenery.

A brief word on the townships: London, Paris and Banana are the principal settlements, the latter named after a single example of that fruit that was once grown here. As you leave its city limits a sign proclaims the demographically unique message, 'Farewell Banana (population 666)' – an ominously diabolical number to be advertising, but there are not many visitors to deter, bar a handful of twitchers, divers and stamp collectors (disproving the adage that philately will get you nowhere). To certain devotees from around the globe, though, this place is regarded as Bonefish Central.

Albula vulpes is perhaps the ocean's ultimate light-tackle species. The name means 'whitish fox', and it is affectionately known as foxfish, bonedog, banana fish or Houdini fins (blink, and it has disappeared). A bullet of piscine muscle jacketed in nickel, it looks a little like our mullet or barbel, with mirrored flanks, an inboard turbo-charger and a highly developed early-warning system for predators. The bonedog is so nervous that many are said to die of ulcers: the least splash or shadow, and they spook away into the depths. If hooked, their run is like the strike of chain lightning and can tear 100 yards or more off the reel – not bad for a fish the size of a decent brownie.

These beautiful, elusive, hydrodynamic creatures haunt the finger channels and drop-offs surrounding the atoll, pale ghosts zigzagging across the sand at that happy hour when the tide runs thin and clear over the flats and they can flush out worms, crustacea and other nourishing snacks of the submarine kind. Just spotting Mr Boney is a challenge: he may betray his spectral presence by mudding or tailing or creating a riffle of nervous water, but often one is reduced to searching for a mere suggestion of a fish, a shadow on the sand, a single gleam, a tell-tale innuendo. Then the cast needs to be long, quick, accurate and delicate. This is a challenging quarry.

So there we finally were, that September, four plane flights and half a world away from England, a four-man fighting unit of Brits, bristling with fly rods and heading for our first bone zone. The officer command-ing our squad was the Colonel, a genial angling veteran, ramrod straight and a stickler for efficiency. Bonefish Bill, the *bashi-bazouk* of the saltwater flats, with a bandana round his forehead and a video camera over his shoulder, was next in line, intent on documenting our exploits, although the subsequent film mostly featured our fourth member – the Maestro – since he was a highly regarded casting instructor. Together we made a mean, keen fighting machine.

As part of my mighty preparations I had assembled a preposterous array of gear (six rods, ten boxes of flies), including a snazzy new Scandinavian Loop Hi-Tech fly reel of which I was swaggeringly proud. This was to be its first outing, and I am afraid I wasted no time showing off its film-star looks, especially the state-of-the-art lever drag system, extolling its superiority over what I regarded as the bog-standard models my compatriots were toting. When fishing the salt, the reel is no longer just a spool for storing spare line: it becomes your most precious instrument. And so (*mea culpa*) I bragged about my new acquisition, and strutted around on deck as if I was the love-child of Dame Juliana Berners and Ernest Hemingway.

The Colonel and I disembarked at the first flat (Arthur Island) and began to wade knee-deep through the deliciously warm sea. Stalking the bones here may be hot work, but it is not physically strenuous: what leaves you pleasantly exhausted at the end of the day is the mental intensity of the experience. You have to concentrate like crazy on a liquid wilderness that can seem otherworldly and almost overwhelming – the endless prospect of a wide horizon where the marine light causes weird striations of azure, cobalt and turquoise, where the long world of the sandflats seems to dwarf you as it stretches to meet the ceramic rim of the sky. This is what I call *pêche extrême*, or fishing on the edge.

We managed to get our eye in, catching twenty-one bones in that first session. They averaged a couple of pounds each, and, though happy enough by the way things were going, I enquired of our guide if there were any places in the lagoon that attracted larger specimens; he said there was a flat we would be passing that afternoon, small enough for one angler to cover in ten minutes, where big fish often grazed. Out of sheer, unnecessary greed I resolved to keep this information to myself, and be first off the boat when we got there. *Mea maxima culpa.*

Now it was all coming together, iceberg and Titanic, 'the convergence of the twain'. I extricated the hook from my thumb and pulled line off my lovely Loop. Moby Bone was rootling his gentle way across the flat, not 30 feet from where we stood – a grey airship. The fish of a lifetime.

How large was he? Well, I have cradled bonefish of over 11 pounds in my arms, and this chap was certainly into double figures (Incidentally, don't listen to people who dismiss Christmas as a nursery for tiddlers: a bonedog of 23 pounds was caught here in 1994). He was the fish I had come for, and I was determined to meet my destiny.

The first cast went all over the place, like a madwoman's custard.

Astonishingly, my fish continued to browse undisturbed. I made a rapid retrieve and threw again; he veered from his course, curled his tail in anticipation and hoovered up my apricot Charlie as it skipped away from him across the sand. As if in slow motion I saw myself raise the rod and strike him (all wrong) like a trout, so that the fly popped out of his underslung mouth. I said something in Anglo-Saxon. But, instead of fleeing the scene, this remarkable fish began to cast around like a hound feeling for lost scent; with my third go I plipped it close to him once more, and he pounced on it like a child lunging for candy.

There are certain things in life one can learn but cannot be taught. Just occasionally the fog of ignorance parts and a glint of intuitive understanding results. A philosopher might call this a metaphysical insight, and the bullfighter knows it as *momento de la verdad*, the moment of truth during which for an instant one can perceive the world with a rare and terrible clarity. Wordsworth wrote a great deal of his poetry about these 'spots of time', but you do not have to be a swami to recognise the phenomenon as one which is occasionally familiar to anglers. Norman Maclean identified this intense mental dimension of angling in his wonderful novella *A River Runs Through It*: 'Poets talk about "spots of time", but it is really fishermen who experience eternity compressed into a moment. No one can tell what a spot of time is until suddenly the whole world is a fish, and the fish is gone . . .'

Fancy gobbledegook, you say? Well, go stick your wedding tackle in a Magimix. One reason angling offers such emotional refreshment to millions around the world is that there is always something to learn, and that process of continual discovery keeps the mind young and at times leads us to brush up against the mystery of Nature herself. When you are out on the water you just never know what you are going to encounter next, nor quite how you will react, however well prepared. In this way, fishing is unlike other 'sports', because the adversary is often invisible and an unknown quantity. To rise to this challenge, the angler tries to cultivate an amphibious cast of mind, learning how to hone his senses, detect nuances, read signs, develop instincts in that ultimately vain attempt to get on the wavelength of the fish. Concentrating on such inner resources, he may at moments discover something about himself in the process.

And these things, surely, are the lessons from the fish.

Here, then, was my moment in the sun: the water, light and air seemed to conspire in harmony, the entire Pacific held its breath, and the only thing that seemed to matter in this brief compression of eternity was me staring at the fish. I set the hook.

When a bonefish feels the steel it generally the streaks for the horizon, the reel making several thousand RPMs. But this one moved off slowly for about 20 feet, then turned and began to run *towards* us. I stripped in line, raising the rod in a high arc to maintain contact, but just then he turned and sprinted for the edge of the flat, 100 yards or so away. Confidently, I stood my ground until, under my horrified gaze, the outline of the miraculous new reel began to swell as great coils of yellow flyline started to blossom from it into an hellacious overrun.

'No good, Dave. Quick,' shouted Tyrone, and we splashed speedily after the sizzling bone. I scrabbled at the tangle during this brief pursuit, and felt a cold clench at my heart as I saw the cause: the drag lever had been set down to 1, about right for a 6-ounce pollack. I had been in too much of a hurry to triple-check.

The bonefish dashed over the coral rampart at the end of the flat, and disappeared into the deep channel beyond. By the time I had unpicked my mess, the tippet had been severed against the serrations of the reef. Farewell Banana.

Shakespeare (the dramatist, not the tackle manufacturer) reckoned that, if you are properly attuned, there are sermons in stones and books in babbling brooks. No doubt the odd brush with Nature can offer you an insight into the human condition, but frankly none of this was uppermost in my mind as the punt returned and I struggled disconsolately aboard, face livid beneath my white sunblock. I blurted out my disastrous news to the others, and of course they laughed. We had caught nearly a hundred fish between us that day, and the last thing anyone wanted to hear was a hoary old tale of one that got away, narrated by a slightly singed Buster Keaton. My life had slid from the sublime to the ridiculous, and I was urgently in need of cool ale.

So what exactly did I learn from my equatorial nemesis? Disaster dwells in the details, and despite twelve months of careful preparation I had blown my main chance through a combination of haste, avarice and complacency. In my rush to steal a march on the others I must have nudged the drag against the hull, so I never did become the hero of the hour. Experience may be the best teacher, but she sends in some horrendous bills.

No doubt that great fish has forgotten me, but I feel sure I will remember him for ever.

Trevor Stewart

The Tarpon, Phantom of the Sea

In 1986 I was given the opportunity to work in The Gambia, West Africa. Having read so much about the virgin fishing grounds off West Africa, my mouth began to water at the thought. But with my favourite pastime engraved in my mind and at times (most of the time) dreaming and fantasising of what might follow, I was reminded of my prime objective when I attended a very sensitive meeting in London. Then, before I knew it, the day had come and I was off to work in the sun, leaving behind a German winter.

My thoughts were not on the job I was being sent to perform, but on whether I had packed enough or even the right tackle to see me through the best part of a couple of years, fishing for species which I had not even dreamed about. Within three months I was writing to friends back in England, getting them to make up various parcels of tackle.

I soon made a number of good friends in the expatriate community who had similar interests. Amongst these was the American Ambassador, who loved his fishing and had a purpose-built Boston Whaler, a craft made to contend with the Atlantic swell. Unfortunately, however, due to his diplomatic duties, he hardly found time to use it, but being a wise man he realised the advantages of allowing me free use of it.

I soon got to know a vast area of the Atlantic Ocean off the coast of The Gambia and Senegal. I maintained a log every time I went to sea, which proved to be invaluable as time went by. I was able to advise people on when to visit and what they could expect to catch. In addition I was able to prepare and publish the expatriates' *Aide Memoir to Sea Fishing in West Africa*.

Every angler in the community kept talking about 'when the tarpon arrive'. Nobody could actually tell me when this was likely to be; more curiously, nobody actually knew anyone who had caught one. At this stage I did not know what to expect of the tarpon, but hoped they would live up to their reputation as the most interesting game fish in the Atlantic. Fish have been reported between 200–300 pounds; they average about 5 feet in length, with a number growing to 8 feet. They are referred to as the 'Silver King' for the scales in a mature fish are the size of silver dollars, and reflect the light like polished metal. They have been seen leaping up to 10 feet clear of the water when hooked.

While we were waiting for the tarpon to show, the monsoon season arrived. One of the young Gambians I had been teaching got to know of my love for fishing and proudly announced that his family were all fisherfolk who lived in a village on the Gambia river. Having spoken to his family one weekend, he arranged for me to visit his village to talk of my experiences. Little did I know that angling technology had passed this part of the world by. Needless to say my tackle supply was further depleted in the hope that my new friends would benefit from some of the high-tech patterns of the many hooks and swivels which I gave them. They did, their catches increased, as did their wealth.

I was soon introduced to the rudiments of local boat fishing, as my next visit to the village was in response to an invitation to fish with my friend's family. Little did I know that I was about to take my life into my hands. Armed with my usual array of rods and tackle box, I set off for the village, an expedition in itself, as all the roads had been washed away during the recent monsoons. On arrival at the village I was met with raucous laughter as I unpacked my tackle. I wondered why. I was then taken to the river and shown the dug-out canoe which was my craft for the day. It was about 20 feet long and had a beam of 20 inches, and was fitted with a stabilising outrigger and a 20-horse-power outboard engine clamped to the stern. I had gone past the point of no return and, not wanting to offend the family, prepared myself for the day's fishing. Space being somewhat restricted, a quick rethink was needed as far as tackle was concerned. I now understood the reason for the laughter. Armed with my old faithful Ugly Stick and ABU 7000, loaded with 20-pound monofilament and a bag containing various bits of terminal tackle, we set off down the river to the open sea.

I have never been so scared in all my life as I was that day; I was terrified to move while we were motoring, for fear of capsizing the craft. Within an hour we were out of sight of land; instinct determined when we were at the desired fishing ground. I thought it strange that the craft did not carry an anchor or any means of anchoring. The two local men unravelled their hand lines of 200-pound monofilament, which had seen better days. The business end consisted of a weight of about 4 ounces and a short snood of 12 inches with a 12 'O' + sized hook! I had nothing in my bag to compare!

The boat drifted gently on a slight Atlantic swell. Within an hour a bite registered on one of the hand lines, and the Gambian started to move it in small jerking movements in an attempt to entice whatever fish was becoming interested in his bait. Following another bite he started to retrieve his line steadily into the boat when suddenly line was ripped from his hand and streamed out from its neat coil in the bottom of the boat until it came to the end where it was tied to a rather crude cleat.

What followed was magnificent! The boat started to move down tide under the pressure of whatever was on the end of the line, which by now was as taught as a violin string. The angle of the line rapidly decreased, then suddenly 100 yards behind the craft, a sailfish leaped into the air and proceeded to tail walk – a marvellous sight, never to be forgotten. The fish was soon tired and was lashed to the outrigger. My thoughts were on also catching a sailfish and I was soon rewarded. The ensuing battle on my 20-pound outfit lasted for nearly an hour. I am not sure who was more tired, the fish or me; it must have made at least a dozen runs for freedom, managing to strip off more line than I thought I had on the reel. Having unhooked the fish I held it in the tide by the side of the boat for a few minutes, and with a flick of its sickle-shaped tail it glided away into the depths. Shortly after my catch we returned to the village. Nobody spoke a word, but I am sure I could read the villagers' thoughts. I appreciated my experience in the traditional craft but, despite being overcome when I caught my first sailfish, should the opportunity arise again to venture into the unknown to fish the unknown in an unknown craft, I would be tempted to decline.

All through 1986 not a tarpon was seen or heard of – at least from any reliable source – and I was beginning to think of it as a phantom. Easter 1987 saw most of the expatriate community assembled in the British High Commissioner's residence for a charity cocktail party. The residence was beautifully situated on top of a 160-foot cliff overlooking a rocky outcrop bounded by deep water. One member of my group was staring out to sea, when he saw what he thought was a school of dolphins, heading close into the rocks. The High Commissioner proudly produced his binoculars for me to have a closer look. I knew they were not dolphin and felt sure they must be tarpon, about thirty of them basking in the early evening sun.

For a number of the guests the cocktail party was cut short as we departed to launch various small boats, armed with rods and tackle.

Despite a number of takes, not a single fish was landed; as soon as the fish had thrown hook, it would proudly return to basking mode. It appeared that they were playing with us. That evening a number of us got together to discuss and display all the various methods used to tempt our prey. Not one of the assembled anglers, all of different ability, had previously landed a tarpon.

Not wanting to admit defeat, we spent many hours subsequently planning our next attempt. Yet again a number of fish were hooked and threw the hooks after powerful leaping runs. Were we to be beaten? No! The following evening I hooked into a fine specimen of 94 pounds; the frenzied fight which ensued confirmed the reputation of the 'silver king'. I was fortunate to land this, my one and only fish. I am sure that one fish was our quota, because just like the wind, the following day the tarpon left the area, possibly to move further down the African coast to taunt other expatriate angling communities.

Jim Whippy

I Know Nothing

A ngling cannot be learned during one summer's fabulous fishing on a mark full of fish. It will not be mastered in a winter blessed by whiting galore and double-figure cod. A knowledge of angling can only be acquired by piecing together, season after season, the complex trends and seasonal changes brought by moon, tide, temperature and a host of other variations on a theme. Every year the fish are drawn by instinct to migrate, spawn or follow the food chain, and only experience will tell us, broadly speaking, when and where this might occur. So many things can occur that can slightly change the pattern, leaving us to scratch our heads and go back to the drawing board.

Various incidents come to mind when my years of angling knowledge were brought into question by the fish deciding to follow their own instincts and not doing as my experience forecast they would. The first two were close to home, where the quarry was those impressive, silver-scaled beauties, the bass; and the third showed up a lack of experience with a hard-fighting game fish.

The sea was oily calm, and the warm July sun twinkled on the surface as I anchored up near a small wreck a few hundred yards off the Sussex coast. My wife Pat had come with me in our 12-ft dinghy for a crack at the big bass that move in with the flooding tide. On the twenty-minute trip along the coast to the mark, we had trolled a set of silver shrimps, but had only picked up a couple of mackerel. These were filleted down to make long thin strips, hooked just once in the end so they would move in the tide to emulate a sand eel. We cast near the wreck with a 1-ounce arlesey bomb. Apart from the odd crab nibbling the ends of the bait, the rods resting on the gunwales remained motionless. It is a mark we normally only fish for a couple of hours and as bait was in short supply I was soon baiting up for the last cast. Pat pointed to the remains of one of the mackerel that was just a head and guts with every bit of flesh carefully removed, 'I'll use what's left,' to which I replied, 'No, you'll only get one of those small congers if you do.' It had happened many times before on this mark.

The bait had not been in the water for more than two minutes when the rod keeled over and line peeled off the reel in what was a typical bass run. Several anxious minutes later, a beautiful bass came to the surface, and as it shook its head back and forth we could see that it had that golden glow around the gills which only a mature fish nearing double figures has – and it was 10 pounds 6 ounces, indeed Pat's second double-figure bass in only two seasons fishing for them. I was still waiting for my first double in ten years. 'Good conger wasn't it?' commented my dearly beloved.

'OK, so I know nothing', was my mumbled response.

Two months later, I was at the same mark, with the same bait, after the same quarry, but with a different crew. My youngest daughter was with me this time. The boilers of the wartime wreck could be clearly seen as we manoevred the dinghy for anchoring. This was where the bass would come with the flooding tide, grabbing any crabs that had not gone to ground and laying siege to the small fish swept by in the tide.

The first fish to show was a small conger of about 9 pounds that took my strip of mackerel, which I managed to unhook and return without any problems. Within minutes Anna's rod arched over and she began to wind in a fish on her 8-pound class gear. My immediate reaction after looking at the dogged resistance and regular thumping of the rod, was that the small conger had returned. 'Dad, aren't you going to get the net ready?' she asked with growing anxiety, as she brought the fish nearer the boat.

'No love, it's only that small conger,' I said knowingly. 'We'll just shake him off when he surfaces. We're after bass.' And I carried on filleting some more bait.

Then, without any of the usual searing runs, a super bass appeared on the surface, 6 feet from the boat. Anna yelled excitedly for the net. I dropped the filleting knife and grabbed the landing net, struggling to extricate it first from a tangle with a spare rod, then from the bait bucket, before it caught on one of the rowlocks and finally the outboard motor. When I eventually got the fish into the boat, we could see it was a cracker.

It went 8 pounds 8 ounces and eventually won Anna, at only eleven years of age, a women's world bass record for 8-pound line class. With her light spinning rod, a small fixed-spool reel and the clutch set so light, in shallow water, I would have expected any reasonable bass to have managed to run off at least a few yards of line; I would have put money on this fish being a small conger.

The saying 'Give 'em an inch and they'll take a mile' sums up how fish will expose any weakness, as they did my lack of experience in game fishing, the first time I fished in the USA.

The sun beat down on our bronzed bodies, its rays reflecting off a clear blue sea as the 40-foot charter boat How 'bout it steamed along the line of slick, where water from two different oceans meet. Fish tend to gather along these areas, which are indicated by the flotsam and jetsam that stretches towards Cuba, the nearest land to the west of us.

'Lunkers at two o'clock,' came a cry from 20 feet above us, where the legendary 'Skip' Nielson sat in his flying bridge. His keen eyes had spotted the gold and green shapes of some large dorado, moving like quicksilver as they patrolled the line of shelter the accumulated rubbish gave them, waiting to ambush anything that came into view.

We were fishing 20 miles off Islamorada, one of the many islands that make up the Florida Keys. As soon as dorado are spotted, a small live bait is hooked on and cast freeline towards the fish. They home in and grab the bait in the twinkle of an eye and rip off 50 yards of the 12-pound line, making numerous leaps clear of the water, but they can be subdued fairly quickly if pressure is applied and kept on right from the start, never allowing them any slack line.

Three baits were cast and all three were taken instantly by big fish, which proved interesting. We moved back and forth across the stern of the boat, holding rods aloft or ducking under lines to avoid tangles, with the fish darting in all directions. It was not long before the senior member of our party, Peter Peck, had his fish ready for the gaff, his vast experience of game fishing all over the world proving too much for a 26-pounder.

Joe Murray and I had hooked a pair of fish and after more than half a dozen spectacular leaps we had allowed them to go down deep in the water by letting them have too much line. They stayed close together, well down under the boat, while we pumped as hard as we could on the 12-pound class gear. Sweat poured off us as the temperature was in the high 80s and we could not relax for a second. We battled with those fish for over half an hour, and when they were eventually brought to the boat I am not sure who was the most tired, fish or man. They were a magnificent pair, mine was a bull with a prominent, aggressive-looking forehead, and Joe's was his mate, a sleeker and more silvery fish, both close to 25 pounds. The victory over such rivals on light line gave great satisfaction, until Peter brought us back to earth by commenting, 'You could have beaten them in ten minutes by keeping a tight line.' He was probably right, but it was great sport while it lasted.

Keith Arthur

Salad Days

In my match-angling career there have been several anglers who have left their own indelible mark on me. Some have taught me skills that I would possibly never have picked up on my own, others I have learned from in a different way: how to go about my fishing, the etiquette of the sport.

No one who knew Bill Harris would put his name and etiquette in the same sentence; most would not even put it in the same book. But Bill taught me a lot.

He was a cunning Eastender, from the roughest part of Dalston, just around the corner from the cosmopolitan Ridley Road, once a Jewish market, then West Indian and now a pot pourri of cultures. I first met him in 1966, at the start of the famous Terrapin match team. He had fished with various East End clubs, including the unique Hackney Brothers. One day someone will write a book about their exploits – someone may even print it!

Bill worked for London Electricity as a cable jointer and ran a black-market operation in copper cable. At the time copper was being replaced by aluminium and the instructions were that unless it was easy to get out, the old cable should be left in the ground. If it came out, it was to be returned to the depot. It *all* came out, but *none* went back. Bill had been issued with a grey handcart for tools, which was frequently bow-wheeled, such was its load of illicit metal.

The good news for the Terrapins was that this copper cable was encased in lead and the lead was the perfect thickness for our newly invented block-end feeders. Bill got his mate Eddie Meadows to make up a load of block-ends and at one stage food took a very poor second to feeders in Bill's larder; the shelves buckled under the weight!

He was a master of the art of feedering. His basic rig was a 7-foot Apollo Ross spinning rod with a Mitchell 300 reel. This was loaded with 5-pound Bell nylon, the thickest known to man and next to unbreakable. A feeder weighing 2–3 oz was tied on via a swivel approximately 4 inches from the end of the line, which itself was adorned by a rusty size 10 'Mustang' hook. Bill never quite got the hang of Mustang. Hooks were kept in a rusty state to prevent fish escaping. He reasoned that if it was hard to get the maggot on it would be hard for the fish to get off! One cannot argue with that kind of logic.

If you are wondering if Bill ever caught a fish, let me tell you he caught plenty! There were very few open matches in those days but on the Lower Thames Bill was a force to be reckoned with and on London Anglers' Association matches he was a legend, along with anglers such as Bobby Gleed, Bill 'Twiggy' Branch and Johnnie Whitehead.

Block-ending for Bill was a means to an end. He was not the most gifted float angler but on the feeder he could more than compete. He loved float fishing though, and frequently got lifts (he did not drive for many years, and that is another story!) all over the country to illicitly poached venues. A favourite was a drain near Mepal on the Fens where he took tench to 6 pounds, a huge fish in those days. He only allowed anyone to take him on condition that they did not reveal its exact location.

Another secret venue was Magistrate's Lake, near Cambridge. This belonged to a local magistrate, who stocked it with rainbow trout for his own fly-fishing pleasure. Bill caught them on cheese for his own eating pleasure.

His great love affair, however, was with the Thames from Walton to Maidenhead, and with its barbel. Bill knew every barbel swim and caught plenty from them. His favourite was possibly Albert Bridge, the Old Windsor A.C. stretch just below Home Park, but in the 1960s it was Maidenhead and Boulters Lock wall.

I spent many days and evenings there myself, both with Bill and with Brian Upton, another pal that I have not seen for years. He had the great advantages of a father with a pub, loads of money and a car!

Brian and I fished with fairly sophisticated tackle, 12-foot Apollo Taperflash rods and Allcocks Match Aerial reels, the latest fashions. We 'laid on' under the rod end with crowquill floats and as much shot as was needed to keep the bait tight on the bottom over copious amounts of maggots fed by a brass bait dropper. We used 2.6-pound Bayer to a 16 Gold Stilletto hook.

Harris did not. He had an Apollo Championship rod. What championship it was named after I cannot be sure but it seemed more worthy of weightlifting than fishing. Bill's reel was a Speedia and it was loaded with – yes you've guessed it – Bell nylon, but as barbel were big it was 6-pound breaking strain. No messing about with our pouffy gear. It was a 'cork on crow' float (known as Toppers today), and a drilled bullet stopped with a BB (all shot to Bill were BBs, either big BBs, swanshot or AAA, or small BBs, BBs themselves or no. 4s). The hook was a 'trusty rusty' as they became known, a size 6 'Mustang'. The pattern was in fact 31380, for anyone keen to try the method.

This would be loaded with three maggots unless dace proved to be a nuisance, when the ration would be cut to double, then down to single. You would never believe the number of 6-ounce dace, 1-pound roach and 2-pound chub that used to fall for this – between the barbel of course. No matter how hard Brian and I tried, if we caught more barbel than Bill he caught bigger fish. If we caught a big one he caught loads.

Apart from barbel Bill had two other loves: golden labradors called Sam and salad sandwiches. He had at least four Sams to my knowledge. They shared his life. They slept in his bed, ate his food and went everywhere with him except fishing. They had various idiosyncrasies – maybe a missing eye or an absent leg. This made them all the more adorable to Bill and I am sure one could have taken anything from him but his dog.

His salad sandwiches were something else. He was down at the bakers in 'the Ridley' at six o'clock for a fresh long tin loaf. Bill would possibly get six slices from it, no more. Half a pound of best butter would then be shared out amongst the doorsteps and they would be laid end to end. On three of the slices (the sandwich bottoms) would go a hunk of boiled bacon (only posh people had ham!). On top of that would go a lettuce leaf, followed by onion (spring or Spanish, according to season), tomato, beetroot (boiled to destruction by Bill in his hemp saucepan) wedges of cucumber and salad cream. Each one would then be put in its own brown paper bag and despatched to a Barbour coat pocket. They would be taken out at various times of the day and eaten. It was a sight to behold. Bill had just the two teeth, unfortunately in opposite corners of his jaw; the sandwiches were literally sucked to death.

One famous evening on the wall the barbel were really having a go. We had been joined by two more Terrapins, John Wade and Mickey Lambert, two of the funniest people I have ever met. I still see Mickey occasionally and we just burst out laughing automatically. Bill was fishing in his favourite swim, opposite the lions in a garden on the other bank, and although fish were feeding Bill decided it was grub time. He stealthily slipped the 5-inch-thick sandwich from his pocket, shoved as much of it into his mouth as he could and pulled. At that precise moment his float disappeared, the rod tip buckled and line – I would say it streamed from the reel, but several trips' accumulation of maggot dust in the works meant it ground its way out.

Bill looked at the sandwich, looked at the rod, looked back at the sandwich again and put his rod down, delicately planting a size 11 welly on it to prevent it escaping. His full attention could then be given to the important things of life. When the last piece of lettuce had disappeared and the final crumb of crust been sucked into submission the rod was picked up and a totally exhausted barbel wound in.

Bill eventually gave up match fishing but after he got his own vehicle he pursued barbel on the Thames and even the Kennet. Poaching? Well let us say he did a bit if guesting.

When the electric companies started reducing staff numbers Bill took redundancy and with his lump sum and copper-based nest-egg bought himself a cottage, far away from barbel but near another favourite, the

River Waveney at Beccles. He died a couple of years ago, but all the old Terrapin anglers will remember him for ever.

I shall always treasure the memory of that evening at Boulters Lock and the lesson I learned both from Bill and that barbel; there are right and wrong times to open your mouth and the decisions that follow may not always be easy, but they have to be made!

John Bailey

When Your Fish Laughs

As a child, I loved fish far too much for my own good. With me, fish and fishing was never to be a simple pastime, a hobby, a way of idling out-of-school hours in the manner that other boys adopted train spotting, table-tennis or even rugby and football. Fishing was just something that I could not put down, ever, a part of my life that travelled with me every waking hour and often when I was dreaming.

So great was the intensity of my focus on fish that it is quite possible to believe that I was getting things wrong, seeing their behaviour in a distorted fashion. Indeed, once I had matured to some extent (although this was necessarily limited by my continuing passion for fishing) I began to think that myself. For example, I would occasionally reread my first ever angling article written at the age of twelve with a great amount of embarrassment. The gist of it was that carp were somehow able to appreciate when anglers left their swim and, accordingly, move in for a feast. I believed that I had noticed the big scaly monsters drifting into the margins towards late afternoon when my fellow anglers were packing down their rods, folding away their umbrellas and throwing in unwanted bait and groundbait. Crediting my quarry with extraordinary intelligence, I wrote that they were waiting around the lake, eyeing us from underneath lily-pads, waiting for the clattering of stools and the sploshing of bait, no doubt licking their lips in anticipation and working their pectorals into an orgy of excitement.

To be fair, I tried the experiment several times and concluded that the more noise I made the more this would attract the fish, provided I lay very low for ten minutes or so afterwards. Nonsense? Perhaps or perhaps not. I am now beginning to wonder.

Another article, written a few months after that first, talked about those same carp again in my beloved lake and their behaviour on breezy days when the wind channelled across the surface between reedbeds. I had noticed, with great frequency, that the carp would swim to the head of the channel, position themselves across the wind, raise their dorsal fins like sails and float down the lake like some fishy yacht. Once at the end of their run, they would swim back up, repeat the process and hitch another free ride. I am not quite sure why the paper bought that one, especially as, at the end, I concluded that the carp were showing something akin to a sense of fun. And a sense of fun indicates a brain. And a brain indicates a very competent adversary indeed.

As I say, for many years I viewed both these articles with embarrassment: the idea of a carp waiting for the bang of a car door before feeding or heading to the human equivalent of a ski slope seemed just too much to contemplate, even for me, fish-crazed after all these years.

Two events, following recently upon each other, have rather made me think again and wonder if I was not nearer the truth as a child than I am as a man. Recently, in the course of my work, I found myself by the side of a carp lake in the southern counties. I say 'lake' but in reality it was more the size of the traditional farmyard duckpond, about ½–¾ acre, shallow as the average goose and coloured like the contents of a road worker's tea mug. Let me complete the picture. Imagine this rather undistinguished water surrounded by some twenty to thirty chalets with more heaped up in the background. Think too of its sad little island, crossed by a dwarf-like bridge leading to a bar and discotheque. Finally, to complete the image, picture the dry ski slope looming over all, a Christmas tree of noisy anoraks and shell-suits.

There were some twenty anglers out on the water for the two days that I was there – all with two or three rods in action, all with their bivvies set up behind them even though they had all booked a chalet with the showers, kettles and central heating (for it was winter) that they provided. What on earth, you might well ask, was going on.

I was there as a reporter, to find out for myself. The answer, in a word, was Herman. And who is Herman – or what is he? He is 50-odd pounds of vast, fat, scaly common carp – possibly the largest common carp in this country – a magnet to all those packed there who think huge. Herman had been caught some time in the summer at just over 50 pounds and those around the lake in the deep winter were convinced that his store of fat would have added a good couple of inches to his already portly girth. What on earth would that make him weightwise? A new record? A golden-scaled hippo? A fish of today's dreams, it seems.

As the hours ticked by without any sign of Herman emerging, I began to look at the whole thing in a new light, almost going back to those childhood images that I have already described. Consider that there were twenty anglers with three rods each – sixty lines and baits festooned around such a puddle of water. And remember that it was winter; for most of the summer you could multiply this type of pressure by two if not three. Herman, however, has only been caught on average once every fifteen months or so. Yet he spends his entire life in this network of lines, presumably sliding over them or scraping underneath them or making copious detours to avoid them altogether. The wonder is that he is not bruised or battered senseless by falling carp bombs. How does he possibly differentiate between hook baits and free offerings? Just think of all those chemicals inside him, all those colourings and flavourings and strange essences concocted in the carp scientist's laboratory. What a life! What a world he inhabits. A sad, sad picture perhaps, but just think of what Herman must have learned, of the depth of his wisdom. He surely must be almost Solomon-like to escape capture every day, or every other day at least. What amazing defences he must be able to put up against such a twenty-four-hour-a-day battery at his defences. If one thinks about it, the intelligence I attributed to my own carp thirty years back seems very small beer indeed compared to the depth of Herman's knowledge.

And, of course, Herman is probably no great brain in the carp world either – just a tummy-boy heavyweight. If we accept that he is probably just your common or garden carp of average IQ, then it makes one think just how wise they all are as a breed. Surely they *can* divine when an angler is going home and throwing out free food behind him! Surely they *are* able to enjoy an afternoon's breeze, put up their dorsals and have a little bit of fun. Surely we *are* talking about creatures that have an intelligence that we ourselves can recognise.

Let me reinforce the concept of fun if I may for a second. It was summer 1995, and I was wading some shallows on the river Wye, fishing hard for a group of barbel. These fish were feeding in traditional fashion, moving up and down a shallow, streamy stretch of river over a gravel bottom. The water was pushing through quite hastily, and was about 4 feet deep.

The barbel were behaving exactly as they should – that is forming a solid phalanx of writhing golden bodies and scarlet fins and moving upstream, feeding hard as they went, presumably on my bait and on natural foodstuffs. All in all, they had a beat of about 10 yards and once at the top, they would move back to the bottom and repeat the process all over again. It was this particular aspect that was so exciting.

Normally, barbel move back to their starting point in a regimented, orderly process but not this particular group of fish. No way. These fish rolled and cartwheeled and bounced down the swim at the mercy of the current, waving their fins, flashing their tummies, behaving exactly like a group of naughty schoolboys laughing their way from the tuckshop. The downward journey took anything up to forty-five seconds and the barbel would be all over the place in every imaginable state of disorder but, as soon as the bottom of the swim had been reached, they would swoop back together with immaculate precision and repeat their feeding process. I watched all this, mesmerised, for some three or four hours but then, as the sun began to drop, their behaviour became less excitable, more predictable and suddenly the barbel began to act like any other mature, sensible fish. The fun had gone out of them and the day, for me, had lost something of its sparkle.

So, what are we to make of all this? Was I batty as a boy and am I stark-staring crackers as a man? Should all fish be regarded as commodities, as barely sentient creatures to be caught or dispatched at our will? Does it matter a bean how we treat our fish or how we view them? Have they simply been put on this earth for our stomachs and our amusement? Perhaps these little observations might well lead us to say no. In my view, it could just be that fish are not absolutely unlike dogs or cats for example, able to play, able to work out rudimentary problems and at the very least with a very good awareness of what is going on in their world. I had it right as a boy: fish are special and we would do well to remember that and treat them accordingly.

Jack Hargreaves

Small Stuff and Beginners

This present piece is written by a defeated adult angler. I lie in the grass within a yard of the water – chalk-stream water – and have just finished a letter to a seven-year-old friend, reassuring him of the promise that he shall be taught to fish this summer holiday.

The late afternoon sun throws the shadows of buttercups across the paper and every other sentence I write is accompanied by the sound of three trout rising. Plop – splash – splatter. Without looking up I can tell which is which because I have given these three trout a good deal of time and attention. I cannot catch them. Upstream and downstream more trout are rising, feeding well. And I can't catch any of *them* either.

There are plenty of mayfly – the female spinners are dropping on the water – but the fish are not taking them, nor the olives or alders or capering surface flies. They are not nymphing, apparently, but making clean surface rises. Nevertheless, I have tried them with a nymph as well as all possible versions of the above-mentioned, thrown them the five-nought smut that I keep in the corner of the box, and broken the rules to drift down a wet mallard-and-claret with a fancy jerking motion. All these lures have been presented with the greatest stealth on finest 5X gut. The trout were not put down. They allowed my offerings to pass and went on feeding uninterrupted, and while they continue to do so I have written to say that I will teach my young friend to fish!

Let memory give comfort. The great pike from the deep hole at Sandy Balls; the first salmon in Ireland, caught within five minutes of putting the rod up; the trout that lay under the mill-hatch; the roach in the glass case, stuffed a bit lumpy and touched up with silver paint. We know enough to start the boy off. He must begin right at the beginning, catching small stuff with primitive tackle in elementary waters.

Quite seriously, when children begin to fish very young they should do so with no more than a long withy stick and a piece of line of just about the same length tied to the end of it. I have seen a too-fortunate boy struggling with the beautiful little roach-rod and reel that his father had provided. He was disheartened and tangled, and even when I took off the reel and tied some line to the end ring, the top was too springy and each jerk hung up the wet line round it. A withy stick it should be, or a garden cane with enough taper to allow just a little give. A small goose-quill float. For the bottom tackle it is best to stick to the little hooks that Woolworths sell (or used to) with a yard of nylon attached direct to them. Thus equipped, the boy should begin by catching Tommy Ruffe. Even on grounds of name alone he is a perfect children's fish. You'd expect to find him as a character in a Beatrix Potter book.

The Tommy Ruffe, or pope, is a small cousin of the perch, very similar in general appearance, with the same spiky dorsal fin, but coloured in shades of dull brown and green. At his maximum growth he lies easily in the palm of your hand.

Although localised, Tommy Ruffes are common in places that suit them and these are usually quiet places where a child can make a start without coming up against the problems of running water. On the Thames I have found them in big shoals in the quiet channels between the islands and the river bank. It is here that we shall go in the summer holidays with our stick and a tin of garden worms.

Lesson One – as we are coarse fishing – is to try and gather the fish to us and put them on the alert for food. Half a dozen of the worms must be broken into small pieces – the pupil will have no objection to this duty – and scattered over the water immediately in front. Then ¾-inch of a worm's tail is fixed on the little hook.

The Tommy Ruffe bite greedily and hang on. The float goes down decisively. However much time is lost to the young fisherman through excitement and clumsiness, he will land them without difficulty, and when he has landed one he will want to keep it. The first captive is so precious that a child is distraught at the idea that he might be made to put it back. An earlier young pupil began with a dace and for days he kept it, sick and uncomfortable in a bucket. When told that dace need fresh running water, he took to changing the water in the bucket every half-hour and the fish spent a great deal of time on the grass. At last it was returned to the river to the accompaniment of tears.

The Tommy Ruffe, however, is a good aquarium subject. One of the victims of Lesson One may be established in a fish-bowl, and he will thrive on worms and bluebottles and shreds of meat.

For Lesson Two, some difficulty must be introduced, and it is best to find fish that bite quickly and need striking. In the small eddies of slow rivers – there are ideal ones on the Bedford Ouse above Tempsford Sluice – the baby roach and chub congregate, shoals of them about the size of sardines. There is some movement of the water, but as it is circular the float will go round and round and the short line is still good enough. This time the groundbait will be broken biscuit crumbs, crushed fine with a rolling pin, and the hook-bait a single maggot.

We shall learn a number of things. The quill float will flicker instead of plunging down and at first the child will be too slow to catch the bite. Next he will strike enormously, throwing the tackle and sometimes a little fish right over into the bushes, until at last he gets the knack of a quick but steady pull that one day he will take along with him to the trout stream. A small foundation stone is laid.

As the bites fall off in number he must give the eddy a rest and then sprinkle it again with biscuit dust. Next time round the float can be raised and lowered to discover at which depths the most bites come, and to reveal the truth that the deeper we go the bigger fish we shall catch. One or two of these eddies will do for an afternoon's fishing, and at the end the catch will go back into the river because we are off happily home with a pinch of maggots saved for Tommy Ruffe.

The special delight of Lesson Three is that we shall catch a fish and eat it. A gudgeon. If we go about it properly, a frying pan full of gudgeon. We shall put the withy stick aside and try a rod and reel, though not one of the so-called boys' rods; the crankiest second-hand genuine rod is better than one of those. In fact, I shall lend him my little 7-foot spinning rod with an Ariel reel and a roach line. His bottom tackle will be as before.

The perfect place for our gudgeon lesson lies below Tempsford Weir, above which we have been fishing, just where the little River Ivel joins the Ouse. In the last 200 yards of its individual existence the Ivel is 15 yards wide, clear water running quite fast at nearly the depth of gum-boots.

Early one morning I stood a little way across to throw under the far bank for dace. After a while I let my float run away down the river and as it swung into mid-stream I took a gudgeon. Next time down, in the same place, I took another – and another. The silt stirred up from the bottom by my boots was running down in a cloud and as I stood still to let it clear I saw, 50 feet downstream, a great shoal of gudgeon spread fanwise across the river. The point of the shoal was towards me, with the biggest fish in front.

While the water remained clear the shoal began to disintegrate and scatter, but as soon as I shifted a foot to stir up the silt they formed up again in regimental fashion. In the tent in the field behind me the rest of the family was beginning to stir. I decided to give them a gudgeon breakfast and, in under half an hour, raking with my heel to keep the shoal in being, I collected forty-eight. We chopped off their heads on a log, cleaned them with a thrust of the thumb like shelling peas, and dropped them in the pan. They are not just good eating, they are a delicacy – known for centuries at Thameside inns as Gudgeon Tansy.

That is where I shall take my beginner for his gudgeon fishing. He will stand barefoot in the Ivel, stir things up and discover a little about fishing far off; first stripping off line from the reel and letting the float run down, then later removing the check and allowing the reel to revolve under the control of one finger. And he will learn to grease the line to stop it sinking.

You can find similar places. If you're fishing from a boat, take a garden rake to reach down and stir up the bottom. No amount of disturbance will frighten the shoal. When the Kennet was being dredged with a frightening, roaring mechanical grab, I caught a gudgeon alongside the great iron bucket as it crashed into the water and tore up the bottom.

Fourth – the bleak, the tiny silver 'river-swallow' that darts and flashes just below the surface of the Thames. We will go to a lock a few miles above Reading where a shoal of them can be found on any sunny day snatching at anything that drops on the water.

For this adventure we return to the withy stick with its own length of line and hook to gut. Because we intend to 'whip' with it the float is taken off and a single tiny lead shot pinched about a foot from the hook, to act as will one day the forward taper of the young man's fly-line. Only the maggot is a tough enough bait to stand the strain of what we are about to do, but maggots suit the bleak very well.

Standing with a clear space behind him, the boy will learn to fling the line back over his shoulder and then whip it forward to throw the maggot among the bleak. As it begins to sink, a little jerk of the gut or a tiny silvery flash will give the signal to strike. Sometimes a fish will come right up and show himself, to meet the maggot the moment it touches the water. And thus the seed of fly-fishing will be sown.

That will be a full enough syllabus for one summer holiday, with each exercise often repeated and the elementary lessons understood; and while I have planned it the uncaught trout have ceased rising. They are full and satisfied with something known only to themselves.

I clamber up out of the buttercups and feel the slight qualm of nervousness that always comes with the arrival of the Colonel. He is here beside me, a pretty outspoken Colonel and – more intimidating still – an experienced and brilliant chalk-stream fisherman. Only last week he appeared just as a good fish broke me. 'There you are,' he said. 'You write and tell people how to fish and then, when you do get one on yourself, you lose it.'

I take a look at the hang of his old jacket which usually gives a clue to whether there are fish in his poacher's pocket. It seems to lack bulk. 'Done anything?' says he, gruffer than usual.

'No, I couldn't find out what on earth they are taking.'

He glares at the water. 'I know. I know. One day I'll learn how to catch the damn things when they're smutting!'

So, after fifty years, a fisherman is still learning.

Edward R. Hewitt

The Emperor's Breakfast

Our whole family went to Europe in the spring of 1883, when I was seventeen years old. My grandfather, Peter Cooper, had died that winter, and my mother wanted to get away. We spent the winter in Rome, where the climate did not agree with me, so that in the spring I had developed a very bad throat. As this did not get better with the warmer weather, my mother took me to a specialist in Paris who recommended a course of waters at Bad Ems, in Germany. I was bundled off with my tutor, as I could prepare for college as well there as anywhere. We stopped at a boarding house called the Vier Turme or Four Towers, at the end of the park, by the River Lahn.

After I got into the routine of the cure and my study periods, I had spare time to amuse myself. The Lahn flowed through the centre of Ems, bordered by a fine park which rimmed the river with a stone wall. Just opposite the palace, where the Emperor stayed when taking the waters, there was a stone landing stage for boats. All along the river I noticed men fishing, using cherries, and bread dough mixed with cheese, for bait. They said they were fishing for 'barbel'. This fish looks like a sucker with catfish whiskers. They did not seem to be getting many fish, and I suspected that they had the wrong bait. It looked to me as if such a fish would be more likely to take worms.

One morning I dug some large worms in the flower bed near the Vier Turme, and proceeded with my rod to the river at the boat landing before the palace, as I suspected the drain from the palace came into the river at this point. I baited on a large gob of worms and let it sink to the bottom, as these fish were sure to be bottom feeders. The bait had not been long on the bottom when I felt a heavy pull and I was fast to a large fish. Those I had seen caught were small, but this was quite a different story. My little trout rod had all it could do to handle this big fish, but I finally got it up to the landing and took it by the gills and hauled it out amid the plaudits of the crowd assembled along the stone wall and on the bridge farther up. I was about to hit the fish on the head to kill it, when an officer with his chest covered with medals touched me on the arm and signed to me not to kill the fish but to bring it along and follow him. I was completely mystified and thought I had broken some law or other. He led me across the roadway, over to a large stone fountain before the palace and signed to me to put the fish in the water. Then he was all smiles and bowed me away.

I went back to my fishing still not understanding why my big fish had been taken away from me. It would have weighed about 8 pounds I would guess; it was about 30 inches long. I had not been fishing more than a half hour when the same officer came down to the landing again and touched me on the shoulder and signed for me to follow him and leave my rod. This time I was sure I was arrested and quite scared. He led me over before two other men in military dress and saluted and stood at attention.

The elder of the two men addressed me in perfect English saying, 'I want to thank you for catching me the finest barbel I have ever seen for my breakfast, and I want to commission you to catch me one every day during my stay here.' I then realised that this was Emperor William I speaking, and the man beside him was Fritz, the Crown Prince. I stammered out my thanks for the great honour and retired to my fishing as best I could. After that, for three weeks, the Emperor came down to my fishing place about ten o'clock every morning and asked if I had caught his fish that day. I nearly always got one or two, but never one as large as that first fish, which was the grand-daddy of the river, evidently. Several mornings he asked me to walk with him a ways in the park and he asked many questions about America, about which he was well informed. Twice, on these walks, Bismarck was with him. The old Emperor was always affable and pleasant, but Bismarck gave me the creeps even to look at him. He was the most forceful and sinister man I ever saw.

So fishing can even serve as an introduction into high society.

There were some fine trout streams near Ems where I had wonderful trout fishing with a fly. The owners would let me catch all I could if I gave them the fish for sale. The trout in these streams ran from a pound and a half to 3 pounds, with most of them about 2½ pounds. I used to get as many as thirty on one trip. I have often wondered if this fine fishing is still there.

Martin James

Pike on the Fly

I have learned numerous lessons from fishing around the world over the past fifty-five years. I have become a naturalist, a fighter against pollution, not only of water but also of air and land. I have even helped the Indians of the Amazon rain forest to feed themselves, showing them how to catch big fish by rod and line. I have been involved in helping schoolchildren to enjoy the countryside through the lessons of fishing. But most of all I believe I have become a more caring person. Angling makes you think more of your surroundings and other people. It also makes you realise that fish do not know the man-made rules, just the natural ones, as the following story shows.

I have always wanted to fish the wilds of northern Canada for the pike that inhabit those cold northern waters – not with a plug or a spinner, but on a fly. 'It can't be done!' said many Canadian, American, and British anglers, 'and August is a bad time.' After a chat with Maggi Smit of Go Fishing Canada, I there and then booked a trip for the following August to Wolaston Lake in northern Saskatchewan.

Saskatchewan is the province just west of Manitoba and Saskatoon, one of the two main cities (the other is Regina, the provincial capital), is a lovely place with a fine university, white pelicans on the river, and Wanuskewin Heritage Park, where one can see how the Indians live and meet wonderful characters like Wes Fine Day, a Cree Indian chief who kept me interested all day long with his great stories. The province is the home of Cree Indians, fur trappers, white-water rafting, grizzly bears, caribou, beavers, bald eagles, the loon, and so much more. It has hundreds of miles of rivers and over 100,000 lakes. Wolaston Lake alone covers more than 800 square miles.

Minor Bay, on Wolaston Lake, is a thirty-minute drive from the dusty airstrip of Points North. Accommodation is in simple log cabins and all the meals are served in the main cookhouse. The food there is excellent, as it is at the shore lunches cooked by the guide. No one goes hungry in the Canadian wilderness – unless, of course, they fail to catch a fish. To the best of my knowledge, it has not happened yet!

I had come to north-eastern Saskatchewan up near the border with the North West Territories to fish for pike with a fly rod and a floating line to prove that the big ones could be taken on fly at this time of the year. The sun climbed slowly over the pine trees on the opposite shore of Minor

Bay, just a small part of a lake that is more like an inland sea, it is so huge. And so were the fish!

This deep lake was carved by glaciers long ago and some of the oldest rock in the world surrounds its shores. Fifty-year-old pike swim beneath the glistening surface of these waters and compete to seize any fly that invades their territory. These fish put up a ferocious fight, head shaking, tail walking, and going off on fast runs of 20 or 30 yards and more. The reel screams like a demented demon, the rod tip often plunges beneath the surface. Sometimes for twenty minutes your heart is in your mouth, for these are hard-fighting fish. All the fishing is done from boats: sturdy 18-foot aluminium craft equipped with 30-horse power Evinrude motors, padded seats with back-rests and a built-in wooden floor.

It was an ordinary August day when I had my record-breaking catch. As I made my way to the main lodge for breakfast I was greeted by the smell and sound of sizzling bacon and sausages. I looked forward to pancakes and maple syrup with my crispy bacon. A mist was rolling off the water, two bald eagles were working for their breakfast, a beaver was making its way home from nocturnal wanderings, and whisky jays were looking for an easy feed. Whisky jays are as plentiful there as starlings in Britain, and they will even come down to take food from the hand. We reached the dock just before eight in the morning when the sun had burnt off the early morning mist and a few whitefish were swirling in the bay. The water was as smooth as glass. It was great to be alive. Little did I know what was in store for me during the next few hours.

Corrie Howard, my guide, led the way to the boat, where I stowed my gear; putting on a life-jacket I settled into the padded seat. One pull of the starter cord and we were away, skimming the glassy surface, passing small groups of loons and a lone Cree Indian who was fishing to feed his family and to sell some at market. They are entertaining people, knowledgeable about fishing and about wildlife. But we would return our catch, keeping only one for our lunch ashore.

After half an hour, Corrie throttled back the motor as we made a right-hand turn into a 4-acre bay, just one pin-head area of the vast Wolaston Lake. At the edge of the bay, the water plunged away to a depth of 60 feet. In the bay were large weed beds; hopefully the pike would be at home. Corrie paddled the boat into position so we could drift down the bay; this allowed me to cast in front of the boat for any patrolling pike. Tackle was chosen with great care because I was expecting to catch fish of 20-pounds and more. I used travel rods designed to cast size 9 and 10 lines but Corrie shook his head in disbelief at the idea of pike on the fly.

I was going to be throwing big flies dressed on size 4/0 hooks. Attached to the flyline was 6 feet of 15-pound nylon and 12 inches of 20-pound wire trace; the pike has a mouth full of razor-sharp teeth. I had a selection of large flies but the polar fly tied up by Stu Thompson of Winnipeg was my first choice, for it looked so lifelike in the water. With a polar fly I could imitate the bait fish perfectly.

I cast a long line to a gap in the weed and retrieved about 6 feet of line. There was a huge swirl, the rod tip was slammed down to the water, line shot through my fingers and the fight was on. My first fish of the day was taking line off the reel at a terrific rate as it fought for freedom. The combination of well-balanced tackle and finger control on the reel tipped the fight in my favour. Soon I was able to gain line inch by inch, then foot by foot, first the backing, then the flyline. At this point the fight seemed to be going my way, but the pike was not finished yet; it had other ideas. It dived for the bottom, the reel screamed. I eased off the pressure and let the fish burn up energy. For a moment, all was quiet and then once again I was taking in line. This time the fish was beaten.

Corrie said, 'Well done! It's a good one,' and I had my first look at the fish. It was about 15 pounds and what a fighter – far better than the Atlantic salmon in New Brunswick the previous year. The pike was gently unhooked and released to grow into a 30-pounder. I cast the polar fly again and, as it hit the water, there was a swirl. I lifted the rod tip and set the hook into my second fish of the day. This one was different: it reared up out of the water like a Polaris missile and crashed back in a shower of spray. With the sun glinting on the droplets of water they looked like diamonds. The fight was underway, the fish back on the surface, head shaking and tail walking, then making fast, spectacular runs. With the sun beating down we could be excused for thinking we were on the Florida flats taking bonefish. But this was no bonefish, it was my second pike in two casts!

Pound for pound, these are some of the hardest fighting fish I have caught in fresh or salt water. I wanted more of this action and during the ten-hour session I had it: seventy casts and seventy pike, the best at 24 pounds, according to Corrie, the total weight being somewhere between 350 and 400 pounds. I was too busy casting, playing and unhooking fish to keep count. It was my best ever day's fishing in fifty-five years of angling. I even stopped for a lunch of filleted pike, chipped potatoes and beans, followed by apple pie and coffee.

That day, lessons were learned from the fish. They told us they would take a fly, and in August, too. I had shattered the myth that pike cannot be caught on the fly, and that fishing is no good in August. If that is the case, I wondered, what is it like in the best month?

Tim Paisley

The Two Are Indivisible

I am a 100 per cent addicted carp angler, for which I make no apology. Having said that, it has to be conceded that there are times when I am made to feel an apology – or at least an explanation – is due! I do not think the old school – like my friend Fred J. Taylor and other all-round specialist anglers – quite understand the love affair between most addicted carp anglers and their beloved carp. I get all sorts of oblique – or direct – advice suggesting that I should diversify, go river fishing, do more stalking, or make a real effort to stop being boring and wasting my life on carp and fishing for them. Well, I cannot deny that spending a life in pursuit of carp is a waste, but at the same time there are not enough hours left in that life to do all the carp fishing I want to do at the numerous different venues I have not even seen, let alone spent a few hundred hours of my life on!

On the other hand I have never suggested to anyone that they are missing anything by not carp fishing. I know it is a waste of a life, but then most addictions are, and as carp are now my livelihood it has to be admitted that there are more dangerous addictions. The truth is that through my addiction I still envy the simplicity of a pleasure angler's lot. With a minimum of tackle and a few precious hours each week, he achieves precisely what I require a mountain of gear and two or three days of my time to achieve – fulfilling some little-understood instinct to escape to the side of the water and fish. All anglers share this urge; it is the manner of satisfying it that varies. A pleasure angler goes for a few hours; I go for a few days.

You see my problem is that, to my eternal shame, I am not only a carp angler but a session angler, too. I am one of the much-maligned 'buzzer and bivvy' brigade. My idea of the angling escape is to take my home with me and take root with nature and the carp for a few days and nights. Yatesy will argue that it is possible to carp fish without going to such lengths, and I cannot disagree with him. Others will argue that session fishing is open to abuse, and that some anglers take root for far too long in a swim which others may want to fish. I cannot disagree with them. All I can do is state my case in defence of those session carpers who are not an affront to modern society, and suggest that those who are should be dealt with by means of a sensible fine tuning of the rules.

I would like to make it clear that there was a time when I was a half-normal citizen. I was a sensible pleasure angler, frequent golfer, occasional tennis player, and tended the garden with more than a passing sense of duty. I did not intentionally rearrange my life; the chance capture of a carp started the metamorphosis, and further encounters with carp, carp waters and carp anglers put in motion a sequence of events over which I had little control. Fortuitously the outcome has been that carp and my life have become inextricably entwined, a state of affairs I embrace with an unequivocal sense of good fortune.

I will not throw it open to debate but I do not consider myself to be stupid, which means that for a number of years I asked myself the question. 'Why carp and carp fishing?' I can answer both questions and, strangely, recognise that there are two answers, one for carp and one for carp fishing: the first is a fish, the second a way of life.

Until I caught a carp the species had a certain fascination for me, but the idea of fishing for them had not. I knew no one who was a carp angler, which meant I had no direct influence to steer me towards the species. Like most other anglers I had read the account of the achieving of Walker's record, and was distantly fascinated by both the fish and the circumstances of the capture. The long journey, the camping by the water, the battle in the inky blackness: there was a mystery and an escapism to the occasion that struck a chord, but not to the extent that I tried to make any move to fish for carp. They were distant mysterious fish that others fished for – and very occasionally caught.

I started out as a pond roach angler, moving on to the canals, then on to the reservoirs. To go fishing was marginally more essential than to catch. I was an escapist and a dabbler. Eventually I stumbled upon some nice tench in a local pond, fished for them and became slightly more committed, because to catch tench required a degree of specialised knowledge.

Then I caught a carp. It happened accidentally while I was tench fishing. It was a 6-pound mirror and I have wanted to fish for no other species since. The capture and the carp touched me deeply. Until that moment a fish had been a fish, one roach being much like another, one tench apparently indistinguishable from the other members of its family, other than by its weight. But the carp I caught was not *a* carp, it was *that* carp. I was confused by the capture because the fish seemed to be every bit as much an individual as I am. I sensed a timelessness to the fish which was not based on any sort of pre-knowledge of the species, its history or its origins. I was simply touched by the aura of the fish, and my involvement with carp was consummated by that first unintentional encounter.

I caught that carp twenty-six years ago, some time before Kevin Clifford pointed out that carp are very individual, and that many of them are very old. Because carp are individuals some of them become known, and non-carp anglers tend to scoff at the repeat capture syndrome, which can involve recaptures of a known carp three or four times in a season. Because they are so identifiable individuals are named and become target fish. But the critical bystander does not see the reverse side of the coin: because carp are so readily identifiable, little-caught or unknown fish are just as identifiable as the more obliging members of their family. We now know that it is possible to fish the same water for over a decade and only become acquainted with a percentage of its residents. Our critics tell us that the mystery has gone out of carp fishing because all carp are familiar and have names. The reality is that a handful of fish in a water are caught frequently enough for them to become known; the rest remain elusive, enigmatic and mysterious.

Almost twenty-six years on from that first capture my feelings for carp have changed very little. They are individuals, not just in appearance but in personality, too. I love them all, but – paradoxically perhaps – it is the most frequently caught that inspire the greatest admiration and affection. The fish are resigned but dignified in temporary defeat, fulfilling their part in the angler's imagined brief triumph with stoicism, then going back to fight another day weeks, months or years later. If they are not seen again their obituaries are sadly written by those to whom mystery has to be understood, or solved.

According to Howard Marshall. 'The two are indivisible, the background and the fish.' To analyse the quote is to disagree with it. Because I session fish I know exactly what it means and accept the emotion behind the inaccuracy. There is a dimension to session fishing that sets it apart from most other forms of angling; it involves living at the water. I must have been very familiar with dawns and dusks, sunrises and sunsets before I became a carp angler, but it is possible I had never lived through every moment of one. They are daily occurrences, but I cannot recall that they had previously made much impact on me; and even as a carp angler it was some years before their beauty and significance really moved me. Now I have hundreds of pictures of these beautiful, emotional occasions. On some trips a stunning dawn or sunset can be the highlight of the day – or even of the session if it is a blank – and I will sometimes shoot a full roll of film trying to capture the unfolding moments of magic.

I have become familiar with the full nights of carp fishing now and will sleep during them if the circumstances warrant it. But for the first few years of my carp fishing I found the nights so magical that I did not like to miss a moment of them by sleeping. I am not suggesting that all carp anglers embrace the darkness with the same enthusiasm, but I love carp fishing nights: the experience of living through the dark hours listening to the temporary silence of man and the unshackled comings and goings of the natural world is one I owe to the carp.

Yes, to me the two are indivisible, the background and the fish. Without the accidental capture of a carp I would have remained unaware of, and unmoved by, the cycle of life and nature which is the backdrop to the pursuit of carp. As a pleasure angler darkness was the enemy because it prevented me from seeing the float; dawn and sunrise were largely unremarked and unappreciated because they were too often the backdrop to the race against time to be at the water and in the right swim; and there was a hint of sadness to sunset and dusk because reality was crowding in and another brief period of escape from responsibility was being terminated by the ending of the day. To the bivvied carp angler the passing from day to night, and darkness to daylight are welcome, often moving, highlights punctuating the timelessness of a carp session that is as much a welcome escape from reality as an attempt to catch carp.

What have I learned from carp? Too many lessons to enumerate here, some of which only fellow carp anglers will appreciate anyway. Carp have an aura of mystery about them: one of my first reactions was to try to solve the mystery of their lives, their relationship with their food sources and the environment in which they live. Trying to solve the mystery opened my eyes and my mind, but after ten years of finding that each fraction of knowledge gained revealed vast areas of untapped ignorance I bowed to the inevitable and left the mystery unsolved.

I have settled for spending periods of my life in beautiful, remote surroundings in close proximity to the mystery, and occasionally coming face to face with the object of my addiction. More pertinently I have learned to accept that no writings of mine can do justice to the carp, or my relationship with them. Howard Marshall, who penned the words quoted earlier, 'The two are indivisible, the background and the fish' in his lovely Foreword to *Confessions of a Carp Fisher*, started his essay thus: 'The carp is of all freshwater fish the most mysterious.' Those who do not accept that premise perceive the carp as a mere fish. Those who do, accept fishing for them as a way of life, and I am happy to be one of their number.

Arthur Ransome

Carp

August and September are the best in the year for carp fishing, and it is pleasant to turn to the carp from such fish as trout and salmon which put a less insistent strain upon the nerves. But not too often. A man who fishes habitually for carp has a strange look in his eyes. I have known several and have even shaken hands respectfully with the man who caught the biggest carp ever landed in England. He looked as if he had been in heaven and in hell and had nothing more to hope from life, though he survived, and after six years caught an 18-pounder to set beside the first. Carp fishing combines enforced placidity with extreme excitement. You may, day after day, for weeks watch your rod fishing on your behalf (for you do not hold it in your hand), and then, at last, you see your float rise and move off and, striking with proper delay, are suddenly connected to the fastest fish that swims. A salmon keeps it up longer, but I doubt that even he has the carp's appalling pace. Trout are slow, dogged creatures in comparison. Further, carp are immensely strong. To hold them safely you need stout gut, but to use use stout gut is to throw away most chances of having a carp to hold. There is something terrifying about these fish. To hook a big one is like being jerked out of bed by a grapnel from an aeroplane. Their speed, size and momentum are enhanced, in their effect upon the mind, by the smallness and the stillness of the ponds in which they are to be found.

The pleasantest such place I know is the lake in front of a tower that Cromwell burnt, a placid pool where frogs spawn in Spring, with ancient trees on the still more ancient dam that hold it up. These trees have, during the storms of several centuries, dropped branch after branch into the lake and the bottom there is rich with decaying leaves and fortresses for fish. You cast out and hope that (1) you do not hook an oak bough, and (2) that if you hook a carp he may neglect the snags on either side of him and give you a slightly better chance of catching him by burying himself in the water lilies in the middle of the lake. You cast out, I say! Alas, there is no longer anything to cast for. The lake was drained for its fish during the war and the men who took them took even fingerlings and left nothing alive that they could see. The carp in that lake, however, did not run very large. There were a few big ones killed when it was drained, but nothing of the size I saw at the weekend in a duck-pond that could scarcely have covered two acres. This pond was square and used for washing sheep. There was a little wooded island in it and a sunken willow tree. Its banks were almost without bushes. It was simply a shallow bath-tub of a pond. It had not even water lilies. It looked as if it had no fish. When I came to the pond side, I believed I had been misled and was consoled by watching a flock of wild Canada geese resting beside it. For some minutes they took no notice of me; then, altogether, twelve or thirteen of them, they raised their long, black necks and, a moment later, rose into the air, cleared a hedge and, lifting slowly, flew away. I was still watching them when I heard something like a cart-wheel fall into the pond. Huge rings showed, even on the windswept surface. I watched for a particularly clumsy diving bird to come up again. None came, but, just as a gleam of sunshine opened the racing clouds, there was another vast splash and a huge, pale gold fish rose into the air, shook himself in a cloud of spray, gilded by the sunshine and his own colour in the midst of it, and fell heavily back into the water.

In a few minutes after that the rods were up and the baits cast out (with the helping wind it was easy to get them well out towards the middle of the lake). The floats were adjusted to lie on the surface, held by the resting shot, while the bait with a couple of feet of fine gut lay on the bottom. The placidity of floats so adjusted is like that of anchored ships. Life has left them. They lie, dead, on the top of the water. They do not drift. There is no feeling that they may be approaching fish.

All that can be hoped is that, down below, on the mud, a fish is approaching them. The fisherman can do no more. A yard or two of line lies on the ground beside his reel. Until that line is drawn out he can do nothing. He is immobilised, while tremendous events impend. Chained hand and foot, he waits on destiny. And destiny, rumbling here and there with tremendous splashes of golden leviathans, makes havoc of his nerves. He cannot, like the trout fisher, find expression and relief in lengthening his line and casting over a rise. He must steel himself to leave his rod alone and this enforced inaction in the exciting presence of huge fish, visibly splashing, produces a sort of drugged madness in the fisherman. I could not keep my hands still, nor could I reply sanely to questions. A true record of the life of an habitual carp fisher would be a book to set beside De Quincey's *Confessions of an English Opium-Eater*, a book of taut nerves, of hallucinations, of a hypnotic state (it is possible to stare a float into invisibility) of visions, Japanese in character, of great blunt-headed, golden fish, in golden spray, curving in the air under sprays of weeping willow, and then rare moments when this long-drawn-out tautness of expectation is resolved into a frenzy of action. When, at last, I hooked one of these fish, I could not keep in touch with him, though I was using an American multiplying reel with which, on a trout rod, I have kept easily in touch with a salmon. Again and again, he won yards of slack and yet, when he was landed, he was no glass-case fish, but quite an ordinary carp which, at the end of the day, I put back into the pond. For carp fishing, it was a lucky day. Four times the baits were taken by eels, landed amid anathemas, tempered by the thought of next day's breakfast. Four times they were taken by carp. One fish was landed. Twice the carp shot off with such speed that the reel over-ran, checked and gave him warning. On the fourth occasion one of the monsters made a direct run of 30 yards and then broke me, the fine gut cast parting above the float. There then occurred an incident that illustrates the uncanny nature of these fish. My float, lying out in the middle of the pond, turned and sailed slowly in again to my very feet, towed by the monster who then in some manner freed himself, thus returning me my tackle with a sardonic invitation to try again. No other fish is capable of putting so fine a point on irony.

Peter Stone

Shaken – and Stirred

The little lake deep in the heart of Bedfordshire was a mysterious place. Completely surrounded by trees and bushes, the wind rarely touched its surface; the only movement was caused by its resident carp, roach and tench. The late Dick Walker, Fred J. Taylor and I had taken out a lease, although we knew very little about the fish which lurked in its dark depths.

Fred Taylor and I arrived one hot July evening for an all-night session. On his first visit Fred Taylor had taken a tremendous perch weighing 4 pounds; were other huge perch present we wondered; were there in fact even bigger specimens? Just for the perch alone it was an exciting place. The tench were not large – or at least catches had not suggested that they were – but we did not really know.

On the journey over, Fred and I discussed baits and tactics. With huge perch and possibly big tench present, we decided lobworm would be best. These would be fished under a float in the margins until darkness fell, then legered. Not that I expected to catch a perch after dark. Unlike tench, perch are not nocturnal feeders, but there was a fine chance of one at dusk and first light. Perch feed best in poor light and the hours of darkness would give me a chance of a good tench or possibly a carp, of which the lake held a fair number.

Finding a clear area of bank between two large hawthorns we tackled up. A 6 pound breaking strain line would, I reasoned, deal with anything I was likely to hook, although a very big carp could prove me wrong. But I did not expect one, and in any case I first had to hook the fish.

Finally, with two hours of daylight remaining, we settled down. Conditions were good, an overcast sky and the air warm. All it wanted was a bite from a good fish.

The evening passed without incident. Carp rolled way out and the occasional tench rolled close to our floats. As darkness came I removed the float and recast my lob into the margin, placed the rod between two rests and settled down for the night. The lake, by day so picturesque, now took on a different atmosphere. Owls hooted above us and strange cries came from beyond. One, the scream of an unfortunate rabbit as a fox, stoat or weasel grabbed its supper was recognisable; its short life was over.

It was nearing midnight when I noticed the reel handle turning; somehow I had forgotten to lift the pick-up. I picked up the rod and struck. On feeling the hook, the fish made off slowly parallel with the bank. I increased pressure; still my unseen adversary gained line. I piled on all the pressure I could but you cannot put too much on a 6 pound breaking strain line. Still more line was taken and I increased pressure still further. But the fish continued to take line. Then, quite suddenly, it stopped running and I pulled the rod back. I then realised I was into a very heavy fish.

But what was it? Certainly not a perch. Tench? Possibly, and if so it could be a record-buster. The most feasible explanation was carp, yet the fight did not suggest carp. In truth I had never had a fish take so much line in such a short space of time then stop so suddenly. It was very strange.

Slowly, very slowly, I gained line until the fish was just past the rod top. Five or six minutes had passed, yet I still did not know what it was. But we soon would for Fred had now dipped the large landing net into the water and I knew he would not make a mistake. Minutes later the fish wallowed just beyond the net and Fred turned on the powerful torch. In the light we saw a hugh head with large whiskers – catfish. Seconds later, with not a little skill, Fred slipped the net under 3 feet of muscle and lifted it out onto the bank.

I was staggered; I had never seen a 'cat' before and it was not a pleasant sight. Not only that, I could not hold it still. And the mouth; so wicked, almost grimacing at its captor. With forceps I removed the hook from its row of small but needle-sharp teeth and placed it into my outsize keepnet for photographing the following morning. I do not know when a fish has shaken me more; it was not only the sight of it but the unexpectedness of it all.

The remainder of the night passed without incident; dawn broke and we reflected on the night's events. After a hearty breakfast we lifted the net and weighed the 'cat' the scales showing it at 12½ pounds. Almost without a kick it posed (still grimacing) for the camera then, taking one last look, I slipped it back into the murky depths.

Major G. L. Ashley-Dodd

Camouflage

There are some chestnuts that are so delightful that, although known by all, they will always produce a laugh, and in my opinion one of the brightest of these is the story of the man who owned a chameleon and who used to amuse his friends by placing it on various coloured cushions to watch it gradually change to the hue of the fabric. On his return one day from his Club, he was met by his servant with a very long face who, in faltering tones, told him that Tommy, the chameleon, had met with a fatal accident, and he then confessed that a friend of his having called, he had placed it on various coloured things for his friend's edification. 'Well, Sir,' he continued, 'after a bit we put him on your Stewart Tartan rug, and the poor little beggar busted hisself a-trying.'

My point is this, chameleons are not the only living creatures who can suit themselves to their environment.

The leopard, we know, cannot change his spots, but he does not want to do so in the places he inhabits, as his skin harmonises in a marvellous way with the district in which he lives, where light and shade alternate. The same applies to the stripes of a tiger, or the mottled skin of a giraffe. I remember in South Africa when I had never before seen a giraffe in the wild state, I was going across some flat open country. On my left was a little kopje about 60 yards off with a few wait-a-bit thorn trees dotted over it. Suddenly my Zulu crouched and whispered, 'Giraffe,' pointing to this kopje. I stared, and could have sworn nothing was there, much less a huge giraffe. Suddenly, as I looked at a bush, I saw a movement, which was the flick of the ears of a giraffe, and at the same moment I realised that standing behind two bushes were three of these beautiful animals. The movement had betrayed them, but their colour so perfectly harmonised with the light and shade, that until this slight movement was made they were quite invisible to my untrained eye.

Again, over in Morocco, we were troubled by a lion which used to prowl around camp after dark, as we had a sick camel and he knew it. We were determined to bag him if possible, so we tethered the poor camel out about 200 yards from our camp and dug holes for ourselves at each side of the camel at a distance of about 30 yards. At dusk we heard a lion roar in the foothills about a mile away, and presently he roared again much closer. It was a bright moonlight night and we could see the camel distinctly. Suddenly the lion roared again quite close, and on comparing notes afterwards my companion and I thought it was about to spring on us ourselves. We neither of us saw anything, and after a long pause the lion roared again in the foothills, and that was the end of it. Next day by his tracks we found that he had circled right round between us and the camel, and had crouched and twitched his tail twice for a spring, but had never done so. He must have winded us and made off, but his protective colouring had been so good that we had neither of us seen him, though at less than 20 yards from us. I still cannot make out why at any rate we did not see his shadow.

Animals have not the monopoly of this protective colouring, which is shared by birds, insects, and fish alike, but many of the latter have also an uncanny knack of quickly changing their colour to suit their surroundings. Thus a trout will become in a very short time dark coloured on a peaty bottom, green when among weeds, and very light when lying on gravel. Even the homely pike is a bit of a magician in this respect, and not only suits his skin to his surroundings but can actually change his whole colour in a very short period. Once when a boy I captured a small pike of about 2 pounds and brought it alive to the house with the object of presenting it to a tame otter belonging to a neighbour the next day. Having nowhere else to put it, I turned on a tap in the bath and put it in. When I came to get it the following morning, to my astonishment the pike was almost white.

Take again the flounder: he is white underneath, but on his top side he exactly matches the sand on which he rests, and he has a fringe of fin all round him by which the moment he sits down he fans sand all over himself so that he looks exactly like the bottom and only his two eyes are visible.

Insects too have their own protective ways, while many birds apart from their plumage have a wonderful knack of making their nests and laying their eggs in such a way as to be invisible except to the experienced searcher. In fact, this theme is practically inexhaustible and is one of the greatest charms to the student of wild life. Again, the adaptability of animals, fish, birds, and insects under conditions at variance to their normal modes of life is simply marvellous, though they are not usually so readily adaptable or so quickly acclimatised as the higher animal, man.

Take the common herring: this is a regular sea fish, and if you tried to put him into fresh water he would die very nearly as soon as he would on land, and yet there are huge shoals of herring in the Great Lakes of Canada, which are absolutely fresh water, and on the north shore of Lake Superior there is almost as great an industry in catching them as there is in Loch Fyne.

Pike, rudd, and perch are purely freshwater fish, and yet in Slapton Ley in Devon they exist in huge quantities although the water is distinctly brackish from the sea which filters through at high tides.

On the subject of adaptability I cannot, I think, give a better instance than that of some porgie which live in a natural rock pool some 10 miles

from Hamilton in Bermuda. The porgie is one of the most esteemed eating fish in Bermuda waters, and is great fun to catch if you are keen on sailing a boat. He is undone by his very shyness and cleverness, and the method of catching him is called 'roping'. A bay is chosen for the scene of operations with a fairly narrow entrance. Two sailing boats put out to sea for several miles and then turn and sail back toward the bay with a long thin rope trailing between them. As will be appreciated by any sailor, it is very difficult to handle these boats so that the rope remains sagged pretty deep in the water between them, but the fishermen are most skilled and seldom make a mistake. I daresay motor boats are now used for this purpose, but I am speaking of how they did it when I was there. The water is, of course, gin clear, and when the porgie see the rope coming, they swim in front of it until in due time they are herded like a flock of sheep into the bay: then boats put out from opposite sides of the bay with seine nets, and shortly after porgie are on sale in Hamilton.

Now comes the adaptability of the porgie: this exceedingly shy fish is the principal inhabitant of the Devil's Hole, the natural pool before mentioned, and yet he has so completely got over his shyness that when visitors come there, hundreds of these fish weighing from 5 pounds to 15 pounds not only come swimming up for food, but actually put their huge pink mouths out of the water, and as food is thrown in one can literally hear their jaws snap.

This brings, naturally, to one's mind the well-known fish pond at Logan on the Mull of Galloway, where tame cod are kept under much the same circumstances and fed by hand. This pond is a natural cleft in the rock separated from the sea by an iron grating, but there are not very many cod in it, and they are not nearly so interesting or ornamental as their Bermudan fellow prisoners; all the same, it is marvellous that these fish can become so tame in a short time even with the inducement of food.

The more one studies nature and natural history, the more one realises the wonderful adaptability and natural camouflage provided to all living things by which they are enabled to escape their enemies and live safely in their (often) dangerous surroundings.

Dr Bruno Broughton

Sweet Smells of Success

T he senses that animals possess help them survive in their particular environment and, in most vertebrates, these comprise sight, hearing, taste, touch and smell. Fish gain an additional advantage from the two lines of specialised scales on their flanks – their lateral lines – which can provide them with information about objects moving in the water near by, a sort of 'touch at a distance'.

One means of assessing the relative importance of these senses to different groups of animals is to examine the size of the parts of the brain associated with decoding the messages they convey. In most fish species, the olfactory lobes of the brain are large and well developed. From this, we can safely conclude that the ability to detect and react to smells is important to fish – helping them to navigate, find a mate, avoid danger and locate food.

A well-known example of the importance of fish olfaction relates to the amazing spawning migration carried out by Atlantic salmon. The adult fish live at sea until they begin their arduous journey inshore to estuaries and thence upstream to the shallow, fast-flowing headwaters in which they spawn. It has been discovered that this migration is not a random process; individual fish have the ability to return to the very rivers in which they were born several years previously.

The mystery of how salmon can achieve this remarkable feat was solved by a series of classic experiments carried out by a Canadian scientist, Arthur Hassler. His work revealed that the adults are able to detect and navigate towards the individual odour of their home river, which becomes imprinted on the young fish during the short, freshwater stage in their life cycle.

This fact is exploited by scientists when attempting to re-establish salmon runs on formerly polluted rivers. The juvenile salmon are reared in tanks containing minute quantities of a man-made 'smell' before they are released in the sea. The designated home river is then selected and labelled with the same smell, with the consequence that, in later life, the adult salmon are hoodwinked into returning to an area which they have falsely memorised as their own birthplace.

There is a gathering body of evidence that other species are capable of such chemical imprinting. Indeed, this ability may help to explain how fish in large bodies of still water, and in the sea, are able to locate their spawning grounds with unfailing accuracy year after year. Once there, their sexual behaviour may be assisted by the release of pheromones, or 'sex smells', which help to synchronise the mating process. Certainly, with one type of diminutive sea fish, the blenny, it has been shown that male fish kept in a tank will react to the introduction of water from another tank containing females by changing into their breeding colours.

In detecting the presence of danger, this sense of olfaction can play an important role in the survival of fish. The German scientist and Nobel prize winner Karl von Frisch discovered the presence of so-called 'alarm substances' in the skin of several fish species. He deduced that the release of these odours from a wounded fish may serve to alert the rest of the shoal to the presence of danger of which they might otherwise be unaware.

A simple fish-tank experiment will confirm, for instance, that minnows undergo frenzied behaviour when the mucus from one of their predators, pike, is introduced into the tank. However, in this case the response is not innate – minnows which have never been in contact with pike fail to react in this manner.

Olfaction as a means of finding food undoubtedly occurs in many, if not most, fish species, something which anglers will readily acknowledge. Man's use of attractive smells to help him catch fish is not new, though. In his 1676 book *The Compleat Angler*, Izaak Walton makes reference to 'pastes made with honey or with sugar which, that you may the better beguile this crafty fish, should be thrown into the Pond or place in which you fish'.

Since then, anglers have searched for secret elixirs which will improve their catch rates, and our forefathers swore by all manner of additives, such as tar, aniseed and even saliva, to entice fish.

Today, many coarse fishermen – especially those seeking large carp – lace their baits with all manner of natural and artificial smells, and many of the flavours used for commercial purposes can be found in the bait stores of avid carp anglers. Quite what Izaak Walton would have made of concoctions smelling of mown grass, wedding cake, bubble gum and maple cream is hard to imagine!

Outlandish though these and many other apparently artificial flavours may appear, there is no denying that they can help anglers catch fish. This indicates that fish are just as capable of responding to attractive odours or flavours as humans, even though they could never have encountered them in real life. Primeval man can have had no intuitive knowledge of the smell of freshly ground coffee, chocolate or potato crisps, but neither he nor most of us nowadays would have needed lessons before associating these odours with edible food.

Another avenue for exploration is to mimic the natural smells to which fish respond. In many instances, this recognition can be traced to the presence of certain amino acids, the 'building blocks' of proteins – a phenomenon which is common to many fish. As a result of careful experimentation, much of it conducted in Canada and Japan, we now know the key amino acids which will incite feeding behaviour, and this has important commercial implications.

For example, Japanese commercial eel fishermen use short-necked clams to lure eels into their traps, the fish being attracted by the smell emitted by the shellfish. The odour was subjected to detailed chemical analysis, and scientists were able to concoct a near-identical mixture of amino acids which performed the same function admirably and much more conveniently.

This type of smell recognition can help fish avoid other, non-piscine predators. During an expedition to the Arctic Circle, a party of scientists observed how polar bears would capture salmon by waiting alongside the rivers up which they were migrating. As fish passed by, the bears would grab them in their paws, usually with success. However, juvenile bears were less adept at this, and the scientists noticed that salmon would remain downstream of any bear which was inexperienced enough to leave its paw immersed in water.

Why this occurred was discovered following an attack on their campsite by a polar bear, which they were forced to shoot and kill. One of its paws was removed and subjected to study on the scientists' return home after the expedition. It was found that the sweat glands on the bear's paw were releasing a cocktail of chemicals – and that one, a particular amino acid, was highly detectable by salmon.

It is tempting to conclude that there may be a perfectly logical explanation why some anglers seem blessed with 'good luck' whenever they go fishing: if their hands are clean and sweat less than those of their unsuccessful companions, the baits they handle may be untainted with odours which are unattractive to fish. Conversely, some fish may be able to differentiate between the smells of male and female anglers, finding the latter more attractive. Professor Peter Behan of Glasgow University has been quoted as saying: 'It seems quite possible that they [salmon] could sense the sex hormones of women and be attracted to them.'

Difficult though it may be to take this extraordinary statement seriously, it is noticeable that many women are more successful at the sport than their male counterparts. For male anglers, the moral may be to ensure that you wash your hands *before* you go fishing and to ask your wife or girl friend to hook on your bait for you!

Brian Clarke

Case History

I t is no longer fashionable to put fish into glass cases – or at least it is not as fashionable as it used to be. Most people feel these days that the best place for a fish is swimming free in the water. Indeed, in some places now, to kill a coarse fish is a hanging offence.

The Ayatollah-style absolutes which prevail in such quarters are not for me. If I were perch fishing and there were plenty about and I wanted a perch for the pot – perch are excellent to eat – I would not hesitate to take one. Similarly with a zander or an eel or for that matter a few gudgeon. But still, in the main, the best place for a fish – and the only place for an inedible fish – is in the water. This is why the great majority of coarse fish we see in glass cases, were caught long ago.

It is different with game fish. Taxidermists do a steady trade in mounting game fish, and especially in mounting trout. Given that most trout have been stocked and that all trout on some put-and-take fisheries anyway have to be killed, there is no reason at all why an angler pleased with a particular fish should not preserve it. Personally, I have no problems with the occasional wild trout ending up in a glass case too.

What I do feel is sad is the way that so many fish in glass cases are reduced to mere furniture. Sometimes the fish hangs there in utter anonymity, with not even its size or captor being recorded. In some instances size and captor are there, in others date and place are noted, too. But nothing more. There is just the glass and some gold leaf and the great fish suspended and lost. A sublime creature has become merely an object; the highlight of some angler's life is a line of gilt, revealing nothing.

Yet who has never looked up at some leviathan looking down and not wanted to know more – not just when and where and by whom it was caught, but how? Did this awesome prize come out of the blue or was it a known fish, hunted and stalked? How did it take? What did it take? What was the angler's reaction when he realised he had hooked it? What was the fight like, if that was exceptional? Was there anything other than the fish's great size that made its capture stand out? For all that some anglers keep detailed diaries, a diary does not follow a cased fish around. Many a fish in a glass case outlasts its captor and when he goes all that made the creature real is lost.

I have only put one fish into a glass case and that was a trout. When I caught it and decided to have it mounted, I determined to record for good what for me were the essentials: not only the fish's details but the detail of its capture. It was, after all, a story which included one of the most electrifying moments of my fishing career. That moment was as linked to the fish as the fly which seduced it. I wanted to preserve them both.

The fish is on the wall above me as I write. It is in a bow-fronted case bordered in black and gold. The gold-leaf lettering records the date the fish was caught, the river it came from, the fish's weight and the fact that, it really was caught by me.

But there is more. Set into the back of the case, as they sometimes are, is the fly on which the fish was caught. That is just above the great trout's head. Set into the back of the case just above his tail, is a small card with his story. Not the whole story – there is a limit to how much can tastefully be fitted onto the back of a glass case, even the back of a glass case made to hold a river-caught brown trout weighing 5 pounds 7 ounces – but still there is the moment of my first sighting of the fish: what it did, what I did and what it did next.

And that moment. The card is the same colour as the back of the case so that it does not intrude. From time to time I reread it and the whole afternoon comes flooding back. The fish in my case becomes a living thing again. The lesson I have learned lives on.

It was a hot afternoon in August 1980. I was on a small river in Hampshire and the water was as clear as gin in a glass. It was full of fish – grayling and trout – but on that blazing day there was no hope of a rise.

I had been there before and once, in that place, between the alders and just upstream of the willow that trailed a branch in the water, I had seen a great fish. It was under the far bank where the water was deeper. Even as I saw it, the fish saw me and left. It was quite unhurried. It had simply registered that I was there and swum away, part real fish broken by slippages of light, part dark shadow on the stream bed, heading upstream. When I lost sight of it, it was heading towards the old mill and the safety of the deep pool in which, presumably, it lived.

The original sighting of that fish was, that blazing day, mere memory. I knew that a great fish probably lived in the deep pool some way upstream and that I had once seen it here, in this place; but that was not uppermost in my thoughts: I was simply fishing and aware.

A few yards upstream of the fallen willow branch I saw a small shoal of grayling and a couple of trout. As I watched, deep in cover, they seemed to tense in the water. I cannot say exactly what it was and 'tense' seems an odd word to apply to fish, but it was something like that; a kind of rigid fin-quivering which was followed, almost at once, by a distinct agitation. The grayling slid this way and that. A trout dropped downstream a yard or two, jack-knifed around in a tight half-circle and faced upstream again, riding a thread of current, sharp-edged.

At first I thought that I had spooked them and froze. A few moments later two other trout came swimming downstream towards me. They stopped abruptly almost opposite, turned to face the current and drifted edgily from side to side. Some of the grayling backed downstream and joined them. No, it could not be me. Something was up.

Then he came, close to the far bank, close to the bottom. He was a monstrous fish, the biggest trout I had ever seen in a stream. He seemed to fill up the water. He was not hurrying downstream, he was mooching; shrugging towards me in a heavy-shouldered, nonchalant kind of way. He reminded me – his effect on the other fish around him reminded me – of some old-time Hollywood hood. Here comes Mr Big. Look out!

The smaller fish moved aside to give him passage and then, when he was still a few yards upstream from where I stood crouched and tense, he stopped and turned to face the direction from which he had come.

I had just changed my fly because the willow branches had reached out to acquire the only lightly-weighted shrimp I had in my box. The fly on the leader now was a small, weighted corixa, the next best thing I had for water of that pace and depth. I unshipped the fly from the ring it was held on, lengthened a few yards of line and cast. The fly went a few feet upstream of the fish, exactly where I intended. As it went in I saw him move forward a little, just far enough to make him difficult to see and to take his head into a patch of reflected light.

I thought he probably had the fly. He had to have it, moving that way, just then. I hesitated. I was not sure. He might not have it. I dared not strike for fear of spooking him in that clear, shallow water and so, trying to tighten gently, I lifted the rod a little instead. It was a tentative enquiry, no more. Too tentative!

What happened next was the kind of transient moment that could so easily have been forgotten, but for the note in the case to remind me. As the rod came up, the line lifted in a drooping diagonal towards the fish. Then it trembled. I saw it tremble and then felt – I can feel it now – a series of tiny clickings and catchings coming right down the rod, into my hand. It could have been caused by any one of a thousand things, but I knew instantly what it was. I have seen the image many times in my mind's eye since: the fish's mouth opening and closing and then opening again to let this strange thing go, the tiny hook tripping and catching through those great, curved, needle-pointed teeth. And then the line fell free. It was an extraordinary split second. The back of my neck prickled. Goose-bumps come up on my arms. The disappointment was a physical weight. I had fluffed it.

I froze and stared at the place. There was no bow-waving departure for the deep pool above, no black shadow surging under my feet. The fish simply drifted tail first downstream as though quite unalarmed. He gave a push with his tail in the place he had been before and drifted sideways into the ranunculus.

I decided to wait and watch. I sank slowly to my knees, checked the hook, checked the knot and the leader and then slowly, so slowly, stood half-upright again. Normality returned. A wren – I had not noticed it before – began to sing again if it had ever stopped. The grayling and the trout seemed to relax and settle. Two or three times one of the trout took a passing nymph.

Time passed. Still I did not move. My crouched back and straining neck ached. I kept lifting first one foot and then another to ease their stiffness. And then, without ado, the great fish came out again. He simply drifted sideways from the ranunculus into open water.

I was ready. I already had the nymph in my left hand and enough fly line out through the top ring to flex the rod the moment I began to move it. I cast at once. The nymph went in perfectly, a couple of yards above him and exactly on his line. 'He didn't have to move,' the note in my glass case reminds me. 'I saw the white of his mouth as it opened, as though he were stifling a yawn. Again I tightened and the rod went savagely down. This time he was on!'

I did not record the rest. I remember some of it vaguely – the bulldozing run upstream towards the deep pool, a desperate attempt to get into the tangle of the fallen willow branch, much splashing, quite a lot of mud, water in my wellie. But already the detail of that is fading because, presumably, it was not unusual enough to be worth preserving.

Yet all the memorable things are there. The fish, of course, to look at again and again: that small head, those huge, hook-tripping, neck-prickling, goose-bump-raising teeth; the massive shoulders and back; the oddly small tail. His details and mine. The fly he took. The story of the events that led to his downfall.

In the great scheme of things my fish is no leviathan. I know that well, important though he is to me. But I would like to think that where he goes, that lesson goes, too. It is just how much has been lost from those ancient glass cases; how the great fish of centuries have been reduced to mere objects and how the triumph felt by their captors has been lost for good.

If only some commentary had been mounted beside them, then some of the high points of history might have been thrilling us still.

Len Colclough

No Fish in Florence

Thetwo old men, grey and grizzled but wiry as terriers, relaxed on a bench they had built for themselves near their homes on a gentle hillside. Naples lay before them, partly shrouded by the mist of an early September morning. The sounds of the city could not reach them; only the rumble of a German truck on the rutted road beneath them caused an exchange of glances and a tightening of cheek muscles. Once, when a convoy of five trucks rumbled northwards, there was an intake of breath and a shared smile or two. These were to grow wider days later when the Fascist Grand Council dismissed Mussolini and capitulated to the Allies, for this was 1943.

'Soon we shall be fishing again, my friend,' said Will, the older of the friends, his head tilting to the right and the Volturno river a few miles to the north. 'The pike will come out of hiding for us.'

His friend grunted and felt his stomach. 'You remind me of my hunger and those German trucks running away with all our food,' said Giordino grimly. But the thought of being able to fish again cheered him and he recalled the taste of *Luccio alla marinara* after his catch had marinated in olive oil and wine, then simmered with onions, celery, and carrots.

Will nodded, sharing the thought and the hunger. 'If only we could go to the market for a little swordfish and mozzarella, then we could make a great *Pesce spada ripieno*. If we had the brandy,' he added, 'and we could wash it all down with a few bottles of Lacrima Christi, if the Germans have left us any.' He glanced ruefully behind him toward the vineyards of Campania, sadly neglected through the absence of young workers.

The two old men, troubled by a mutual hunger sharpened by memories, eased their thinning bodies from the bench, stretched, and set out down the hill toward Naples. For a while they walked, then got a lift on a cart to the outskirts of the city, then walked again, thinking to themselves of the job to be done. Will had been christened Antonio but long ago had decided to prefer Shakespeare to Stradavari because of a lack of musical talent and a hatred of a cousin's violin playing. 'The surnames mean the same,' he would explain to a puzzled listener, 'a guardian of the road, a toll collector, and I do not like the name Antonio, anyway.'

His friend Giordino Adriano liked his name. Once it had been displayed proudly outside the best shop in Naples, but the war had come and taken away the business and four of his five sons. The fifth son had left earlier, during the rise of Fascism, and was thought to be in England. Giordino hoped the boy would return one day and restart the business, putting the vegetables at the front of the shop and the tinned goods on the shelves behind. Perhaps there would be a grandson who would be the best grocer on the world. 'Well, why not?' he said aloud, bringing a cautious glance from Will.

The old men neared their destination, slowing as two German soldiers rushed from a doorway to a grey motorcycle and sidecar, arms laden with cheap cardboard boxes. There were too many for the sidecar; one fell and split open on the road as the Germans sped away leaving an untidy trail of garish dresses and lace-trimmed slips in their wake. Will picked up the largest dress and solemnly presented it to a soldier resting with a cigarette in the doorway of the City Aquarium. The young German smiled while Will and Giordino slipped past him into the cool interior, along an unlighted corridor to a door marked PRIVATE. Reaching inside, Giordino took hold of two sacks containing a pickaxe and a long-handled hammer hidden there a week earlier.

Will took the hammer from its sack and led the way to the aquarium's main rooms, where fish of all sizes and colours stared unblinkingly at them from their huge, dimly lighted windows in the walls. The men knew their targets and Giordino stood by the display marked GRONGO, his feet apart and the pickaxe poised over his right shoulder. The great conger eel seemed interested and coiled closer to the glass.

'Now!' Giordino swung the pickaxe. The point thudded against the window which did not break. Another thud, this time as Will's bigger window resisted the hammer blow.

'Again!' Another thud from the hammer but a duller sound from the pickaxe followed swiftly by a shattering of glass, a welter of saline water, and suddenly the room was a tumultuous uproar of splashing, writhing fish muscle aquaplaning across the floor, mouth agape at the unknown.

Just then the young German soldier, having heard the blows of pickaxe and hammer, drew his automatic pistol and pushed open the door. He was swept off his feet by the rush of water, his eyes rolling wildly as he crashed to the floor. A yell strangled in his throat as helplessly he watched 9 feet of thrashing conger sliding towards him, jaws opening wider to clamp shut on his left thigh. He turned to his right looking for an escape from this unbelievable horror.

At that moment the front of the large display marked PESCE SPADA surrendered to the hammer in another explosion of glass and water which launched the swordfish at an incredible rate of knots. Across the floor it skidded to sink its serrated, elongated upper jaw into the heart of the young soldier. He died, his eyes wide in terror as the great conger eel held its jagged tooth grip on his thigh, shaking the lower half of his body as a wolf would shake a rabbit.

Giordino regained his feet and pulled a long, folding knife from a pocket. Avoiding the twisting anaconda-like body of the conger, he stabbed and cut off the creature's head. Meanwhile Will took the hammer and dealt a death-blow to the swordfish and used the borrowed knife to butcher the carcass, placing the edible portions in his sack. The still twitching body of the great eel was cut into four pieces and placed in the other sack.

The two old friends looked around as they rested from their exertions, waiting until they had regained control of racing hearts, trembling hands and aching backs. Water and blood still swirled over the floor and eased slowly down the splashed walls. The uniform on the soldier's body was no longer recognisable. One bloodied hand gripped the awful head of the conger still fastened around his thigh. In the other hand, curiously white and clean, was the dress, his present from Will.

Giordino walked slowly into the street and found a deep-bodied pram, both unoccupied and unattended. He brought it back to the aquarium, where the sacks were loaded into it, covered and disguised as well as fumbling fingers could to look like a sleeping lump of child.

'We'll tell people there are twins in there,' said Will as the two old and tired men pushed their way out of town.

They were passed by several German trucks heading north, away from the distant booming of allied guns, some to the stronghold of Monte Cassino, others straight on to the industrial north. The streets were beginning to darken as they plodded on, passing a German army barracks now deserted but for four canvas-covered trucks and three soldiers, one an officer who called after them: 'Which one of you can drive?' They looked at each other and both shook their heads.

'Nonsense!' snarled the officer. 'One of our drivers is missing, probably stuffing himself with seafood somewhere.' The men nodded in understanding and sympathy. 'You take the second truck and follow me. The other two will be right behind you.' He noticed the pram. 'One of you can sit in the back with the baby so throw the pram away.'

So began the long journey north along the coast road to Rome, stopping only to refuel and to bite into hard bread and cheese. One of the Germans stole wine from an empty shop and shared it with the old men. As he neared their truck his nostrils flared and a frown creased his brow. He stepped away gasping, 'For God's sake, change that baby!' Under the cover of the truck the old men pretended to obey the order.

'Take a look at what we are carrying,' Will whispered to his friend. Giordino's gnarled hands lifted away a pile of blankets to reveal perhaps sixty or more framed paintings, some large oils, a few small watercolours, and all obviously originals. 'If the other three trucks are like this,' Will observed, 'they must have emptied the art gallery.'

The convoy rumbled on through Rome, along the valley of the Tiber, then climbed the gradients to Orvieto and on to Arezzo. The old men were stiff and exhausted after 400 kilometres on a diet of hard cheese, even harder bread, and chunks of raw conger-eel which they stuffed into their mouths with one hand while holding their noses with two fingers of the other. The soldiers kept their distance and never enquired about the baby which was growing smaller with every meal. Will begged milk for it at every village stop so that he and Giordino could line their stomachs before sucking on the now very overripe fish.

'Fifty kilometres to Florence!' mused the officer as they rested in Arezzo. The two old men looked at each other and knew the time had come for action if they were to save the collection and return it to Naples. Giordino took out his folding knife and sliced up the rest of the fish knowing he would not be disturbed.

'I'm changing the baby,' he called to the others who drifted away quickly across the town square. Will took a handful of the sliced eel to the fourth truck and funnelled it into the petrol tank. He repeated the operation four more times to the fourth truck and then four times to the third in line, adding a few chopped swordfish bones as an additive to each handful.

Eventually the convoy moved off again winding down the valley of the River Arno which had been netted out to supplement the rations of the

Germans and their friendly Fascists. After 10 kilometres the fourth truck gasped to a halt, the driver not believing the stench when he lifted the bonnet. After another 2 kilometres the third truck stopped with a curious choking sound that might be associated with a cat with something stuck in its throat. The lead truck roared down the winding road, not noticing the halving of the convoy behind him. Giordino kept his vehicle close behind the officer to obscure his vision on the straighter stretches of road.

Soon they entered the city of Florence and before long Giordino dropped back allowing other traffic to separate him from the lead truck. Seizing his chance he swung the wheel hard to the right and sped along until a wider road to the left attracted his attention. He turned the wheel and immediately caught his breath, as many had before, as he saw the Piazzo del Duomo for the first time. Giordino stopped to savour the view while Will came from the back to join him.

'Where shall we go? Who should we tell?' they asked each other and decided that paintings ought to be well received at the Uffizi Palace which, before the war, had housed over 2,000 rare canvasses. They found a side door and banged on it until it was opened by a giant of a man with a great shock of white hair, a red face, and a chess piece in his left hand.

They explained. He came to the truck, twitched his nostrils a few times, and inspected the paintings one by one, muttering all the while: 'Botticelli; Tintoretto; another Botticelli; Caravaggio; aah, a Piera della Francesca!', and so on until he cried suddenly, 'Let's get them inside!' They did, and then sat down to rest while the white-haired giant made arrangements for the other three trucks to be found and relieved of their contents. Will turned to Giordino and began to describe his hunger pangs. Perhaps now they would be rewarded with a memorable meal, a beautiful wine, brandy, even a cigar. The giant began a pompous speech to an audience of two:

'Italy will be forever grateful to the heroes who have saved this magnificent collection . . .' and on he droned, loving the sound of his own voice, caressing every word, until Will interrupted.

'You must not thank us for we are not the heroes. You must be grateful to the fish who gave up their lives to save the treasures of Italy.' Then he asked for a drink and some food.

The big man looked surprised. 'We have no food here but I will show you where to get water.' And he took them outside. Will and Giordino looked helplessly at each other.

'Where is the Aquarium?' Giordino enquired.

'Aquarium? Aquarium? There are no fish in Florence!'

Word spread through the city and further afield. Within a day the whole of starving Italy knew of the old men's exploits. Within two days there was not a fish left in any of the country's aquaria. They were taken, treated like gods, and eaten as manna from heaven.

Tom Fort

Saint Fortitude

The fact that I am, in my mid-forties, so much wiser, more mature and more sensible than I was when I first became a fisherman at the age of eight may have nothing whatever to do with the countless hours spent in the intervening decades with rod in hand by lake and river. But it is pleasanter to believe the contrary, that some of my strengths and virtues – assuming there are any – I owe to the beneficent influences of fishing.

That they are beneficent I trust no reader of this book will dispute. I have in my time encountered a handful of out-and-out rotters when fishing. There was one in Ireland last summer, the worst sort of ignorant, know-it-all bighead whose company in the boat turned what should have been a delightful day on the drift into an ordeal. And only the other day there was a fat fool who, having hurled his maggot-packed swimfeeder within a couple of feet of where I was spinning had the cheek to accuse me of breaking the law by trailing my pike bait.

But generally speaking, I find anglers to be worthy and decent souls, affectionate towards children, respectful to their parents, attentive to the elderly as they cross the road, honest in paying their taxes, and redeemed in their faults by their love of their sport. Surely it is not fanciful to suppose that their communion with fish has done something to shape and enhance these virtues?

Fishing demands a complex range of attributes, among them patience (rather overestimated, in my view), persistence, diligence, intelligence, and a love and appreciation of the natural world and the way it is ordered. It also requires, if anything approaching consistent success is to be achieved, an ability to empathise with fish. Unhappily, we cannot think like a fish, even if we accept that a fish thinks at all. Yet that talent for understanding, whether through instinct or analysis, where a trout is likely to be and how it is likely to be behaving, is one of the factors that separates the masters from the rest of us.

Myself, I am not much good at it. It is a failure of the imagination, I fear. Although I would have no objection to being a fish – a barbel, for preference – my powers of empathy are spasmodic at best. But even I have my moments, those delightful flashes of insight which come as the eye surveys a curl of water, a quickening of the current, a spot where the subtle fusion of movement, light and rock or weed suddenly shouts 'fish'.

It is sobering to fish with someone who has learned their lessons better than you have. I had fished the Eden and Eamont near Penrith for years before my eyes were opened to anything like their full potential. It took an Irishman, rigorously educated by the fastidious trout of his country's limestone streams, to tutor me. Sometimes, of course, the lesson is provided by chance – as last summer on the Eamont. I was strolling, as I had fourscore times and more over the years, past a dull, flat, featureless stretch. The sun was up and the fish were down; or at least so I thought until I spotted a spreading dimple by the far bank, then another. I stopped, studied, and identified a trickle of light olives and a line of feeding trout. Despite the extreme modesty of their rises, they were good fish, including one just an ounce or two below 2 pounds.

One of the troubles with lessons painfully learned is the ease with which they are forgotten – checking one's tackle, for instance. I should not really need to be told, being so wise and mature, that an inventory carried out before leaving home is more useful that one conducted in rage and disbelief at the chosen spot. The discovery of knots in a cast where no knot should be, of a deficiency in flotant, of a mysterious absence of scissors, invariably prompts a firm resolve to manage things better – until next time.

In this sort of thing I am a slow learner, as I am in acquiring technical skills. I am an assiduous student of other people's helpful hints, yet have always found their application extraordinarily difficult. What seemed so clear and comprehensible on the printed page becomes a hazy and intractable mystery at the river bank. That leader which promised to deliver the fly like the proverbial thistledown – can I remember for the life of me how to tie a needleknot, or what the lengths of the tapered sections were, or their thickness? No, I cannot – so I unpick last week's windknot, tie on a new tippet, and hope for the best.

It is in the moral field that I have, I suspect, derived the greatest benefit from prolonged social intercourse with fish. All sports are, to a greater or lesser extent, character-building. But I think fishing is foremost among them when it comes to tempering the steel of the soul. Certainly no other form of human activity that I know of is more likely to nourish the precious virtue of humility. 'Whosoever shall exalt himself shall be abased; and he that shall humble himself shall be exalted,' said St Matthew, who probably knew a thing or two about fishing.

The inevitability with which the pride born of hard-earned success comes to its fall is a painful business, particularly when the pride itself took so long to take form. Let us use the evening rise as an illustration. We all know that, in high summer, the dying of the day is the time – often the only time – when trout feed properly. But they are also maddeningly choosy and temperamental.

In my very early apprenticeship, the only evening fly I had ever heard of was the sedge, so I fished only the sedge. More often than not, I caught nothing. Then I was introduced to something called the blue-winged olive. Fish the Orange Quill, my tutor said; and the trout seemed to agree, for they took it like tigers. Aha, I concluded, I have cracked the mystery of the evening rise. From now on I shall never know again the frustration of flogging away at a riverful of feasting, uncatchable trout. Puffed up in my pride, I went forth to do slaughter – and retired baffled and hurt. Poor simpleton that I was, I had yet to learn that a little knowledge, unless recognised as such, is a dangerous thing.

It has been a sometimes harrowing process, but I think I have now learned to be more humble: not a Heepish, humbug humility, but a true awareness of limitation. The lesson with which I am having rather more difficulty – despite the kind efforts of the fish to instruct me – is the acquisition of fortitude in the face of adversity. I hope I am improving. I no longer weep, as I did as a boy (at least, only discreetly); nor do I solemnly swear to give up fishing; nor do I break tackle nor throw stones into water where I have been unkindly treated.

I still curse, but not with the frenzied abandon of bygone years. When things do go wrong, in that systematic fashion which suggests some cosmic conspiracy, I try to remain stoical – and sometimes succeed. But all too often the scale and nature of the misfortune are such as to sweep away all defences. I can still see that vast trout on a Kennet sidestream, so artfully approached and deservedly hooked, and the clod of weed which a malign force dispatched in my direction with such precision as to render me powerless as it separated my fly from the monster's mouth. And I can still feel the paralysis which gripped me when I hooked my biggest Eden trout, accompanied by the crushing certainty that I would lose it, and the black despair when I did.

I know that when I can bear such monumental injustices with equanimity, with a smile and a song, I will have learned my lesson. It will be time to give up fishing, and apply to become a saint.

Douglas Hulme

From Little Fishes . . .

I have spent all of my professional life, twenty-six years to date, trying to teach youngsters with special needs. Sometimes it has been relatively simple things such as mathematical addition or how to write a sentence that someone else might understand. At other times it has been things much more mystical, such as why we do not (usually) steal from each other, why it is good to help someone else, why it is (generally) a good idea not to use physical violence and other such aspects of our spiritual being!

Never in all those years, however, have I ever managed to impart such knowledge as a child learns whilst fishing – knowledge which passes mere facts and abilities and borders on the realms of something much greater. Let me explain by introducing you to some of the children who have passed through our charity, Second Chance.

We once had a young man who came from a single-parent family; his father, as it happens, was the parent. His father worked during the evenings starting at about seven o'clock and finishing at perhaps four o'clock the following morning. This meant that he was asleep whenever his son was at home and awake himself; Tariq was therefore almost parentless and guideless.

Tariq had two hobbies – or perhaps an interest and a collection would be a better description. As all readers who own a Mercedes Benz will know, the car has a logo on the bonnet that stands proud of the bodywork on a well-engineered ball-and-socket system. Twist these badges of distinction in a certain manner and they will pop out into the hand quite easily. Thus no owner of a Mercedes parked in West London was safe from Tariq, and he had a collection of 250 pieces at the last count, all carefully mounted on his bedroom wall.

From collection to amusement, Tariq's idea of a 'good laugh' was to creep along the banks of the Thames opposite the moorings of the houseboats with a 'Black Widow' catapult and a sizeable ball bearing. If he could gauge things just right he would pick a boat whose hull was of the right material or thickness, and which belonged to a yuppie weekend owner. If his aim was precise, a hole would appear in the side of the boat just an inch below the water line. He would do this on a Monday evening. On Friday evening, he would again take up position with great merriment to observe the owner returning to a boat either resting on the river bed or at best a good deal lower in the water.

What chance was there for a child like this? Past experience would suggest a well-proven and well-worn path of school expulsions, police cautions, arrests, social workers, magistrates, unemployment and a life of petty crime.

Not so Tariq! The pattern of life I have just described was set thirteen years ago. Today Tariq is manager of an engineering workshop, he has twelve people working under his supervision, and just a few months ago he brought a delightful young lady to my house to introduce her as his wife-to-be. He is more likely to be found on the banks of the River Thames these days with two or three children from our charity, as he works as an advocate for them. What was it that broke what seemed to be the established pattern of a downward spiral in his life? As you will have guessed by now, it was several lessons learned from fish.

Through Second Chance, or Foster An Angler as it was known in those days, Tariq became consumed with a passion – a passion for angling. Every moment that was not spent on the bankside was spent in eager preparation for those times. There was no point in wasteful vandalistic activities, it would only keep him away from the real purpose in life: learning how to outwit the fish.

However, such activities can be costly, not just in time but also in money. Money was needed for tackle, transport, food to sustain the new passion. The only reliable source of money was a part-time job, so although it diverted some time from the fish, part-time employment ultimately gave him access to fish of larger proportions from more exotic venues.

The fish had managed to teach this young man responsibility, the value of hard work, organisation and above all enjoyment of life – lessons most human teachers would find difficulty in imparting in small measure let alone comprehensively to a resentful and ill-mannered young man.

John suffered from a growth disease. It prevented him growing at the speed he should have done, which left him at nearly fifteen years of age with the height and stature of a ten- or eleven-year-old boy. He attended a special school for children with moderate learning difficulties, not surprising for someone who lacked confidence and always sought the easy option of not trying rather than trying and failing. His peers in the neighbourhood would make him the butt of their humour with taunts about him attending a school for 'nutters' and using boxes to make himself tall enough to kiss girls.

John was invited for a day's carp fishing in North London, courtesy of Second Chance. The day went well, and there was good support, including from members of the angling press. John caught a double-figure carp, his first fish ever, which he landed in front of an appreciative audience of fellow anglers both old and young. The audience grew larger with the publication of colour photographs in weekly newspapers and angling magazines. A star was born. The boys who had previously taunted him could be heard seeking advice on the best methods for catching big fish, and adults expressed their appreciation of his feat and admired the photographs. A change came over John: a new hairstyle, a spring to his step, a willingness to take part in classroom activities, a nonchalant attitude to being wrong in the belief that he could get it right next time. What a lesson one fish had taught this young man, what a transformation.

Mark was only four years old when his father died. When he was eight his mother died and he and his older sister went to live with his grandparents. At just eleven years old his grandfather died. When he first met Second Chance he had just had his twelfth birthday and was proving very difficult for his elderly grandmother to control, while his elder sister was just about to increase the number of one-parent families.

I have in my possession several photographs of Mark holding specimen fish: a pike, a carp a brown trout. There is nothing very spectacular about this except the expression in Mark's face – and it is certainly *in* not *on* his face. It is success; for the first time in his life he felt successful. Not only that, he had someone taking an interest in him. It probably felt a bit like something his friends' fathers gave to *their* children, but which he had missed out on. We all thrive on success but how does one teach success? I would suggest that unless one is a fish one cannot teach it, all one can do is try to create it. But I have witnessed the lesson of success as taught by a fish.

Lessons in life are rarely gained easily, and can often be painful, but lessons from the fish can teach us about life itself and still be enjoyable, even exhilarating.

Second Chance is a serious social-work agency in its own right. There is nothing unusual about this and there is a myriad of other charities and statutory bodies that can claim the same status, but what makes Second Chance so unique is the role that angling and anglers play in the way it works with young people up to the age of twenty-one. Is it sheer coincidence that the charity has a success rate the envy of all in its field? I think not. I am sure it has something to do with one of the greatest educators of all, the fish!

A.A. Luce

The Fellow-Feeling

The fellow-feeling in nature, the natural feeling between kind and kind, is raised to a higher power and reaches its climax in the mass movements of individuals within the kind or species. The flighting of duck at dusk and dawn, the wheeling squadrons of golden plover in a high wind, the evening exercises of rooks and starlings, the mad, purposeful dance of a myriad spinners on a summer's evening, the buzzing beehive and teeming ant-hill – these familiar wonders show that individual organisms are not imitative machines, but are instinct with some family life and family feeling of a semi-spiritual character that must at times be taken into account; and if we call it the 'psychological factor', we shall not be far wrong; for it is a phase of the Life Force, the *élan vital*, or World Soul, and ultimately, for Christians and other theists, it is the gift of the Universal Spirit in whom we live and move, have our being and do our thinking.

Aaron's rod budded. An account of an exceptional fishing day on the King's River has blossomed out into an outline sketch of a philosophy of life. We are trying to explain the fact that on the 21st day of June, 1939, under angling conditions for the most part adverse, educated trout, usually stiff and cautious, on a public stretch of water rose freely to an artificial fly, named the Coachman, an evening fly with white wing and peacock body, and took it greedily in the morning, at midday, in the afternoon, in the evening, at dusk and to the edge of dark.

Hunger was not the cause. The normal food supply of the King's River was quite adequate; the trout taken that day were well nourished; they were in fact as fat as butter. Two whole minnows dropped from the mouth of one of them; there were plenty of minnows shoaling in the shallows; the stones had their water-snails and the reeds their usual complement of grubs and slugs. Abundance of bottom-feeding was available. It was not hunger that made the trout take the fly that day.

Nor was it the state of the water. No fresh water of any considerable volume had been down for eight or nine weeks, and the water was low, relatively stale and gin clear. Flood water is said to oxygenate the water, and put heart and attack into the trout's movements; and one often finds it so on the Wicklow streams. Three or four days after the flood, when the trout have worked off the effects of their gorge on worms, they come on the fly greedily for an hour or so; but in this case there had been no flood down, no gorge on worms, and yet the take continued all the livelong day. On the state of the water the trout should have been lethargic and cautious; in fact they were full of dash and attack; they leaped before they looked.

If the cause was not in the trout's tummies, or in their habitat, what about the ceiling of their dwelling-space, the air and upper air, the wind and weather? Their ceiling that day was warm to hot, and bright to glaring. Midsummer sunshine, midsummer heat, and nor'east wind – would any experienced angler expect those conditions to yield their best day on the river? I think not. In weighing the net effects of these conditions, we must take them together, not separately. The long sunshine, the heat and the nor'east wind, taken separately, would tell against good fishing; they form a trio of adverse conditions; yet taken together they may have formed a group, not unfavourable. Philosophers speak of the 'composition of causes'; and here certainly we must take the weather conditions 'in composition'. Trout's eyes are sensitive to bright light; and long-continued sunshine, especially with the vertical rays of summer, tends to put them down. Summer heat, especially the sultry heat of a cloudless summer's afternoon, has the same effect. And a touch of east in the wind, as a rule, is a drawback. Now 'compound' these conditions, as the chemist 'compounds' the bitter and the sweet. Think of them together. Put the June sun with its flaming light and scorching heat along with its keen, cool nor'east breeze. How would they *together* affect the trout? The glaring sun on high, shining straight down into his sensitive eyes would tend to put him down, and so would the keen air, stinging his neb.

Taken together those unpleasant effects might cancel out. Taken together the combination of conditions might even encourage him to rise. That summer's day was what is called in Ireland 'a pet day', nature's unexpected largesse. And part of my theory (but only a part) is that the nor'east wind pleasantly cooled the surface water, neutralized the summer heat, and tempered the tropical glare; and that the warm sunshine softened the harshness of the easterly stream of air, and sweetened its bitter tang. The brightness of the actinic rays made every drop of water spark and sparkle like crystal or brilliant; it flashed diamonds into the curl of every wavelet, and fired the iris sheen of the peacock body of the fly and the glint of its white wing.

This 'composition of causes' was part of the explanation, I believe, but only a part; it was the negative part, but not the causing cause. It explains why the trout were not put down by the adverse angling conditions; it does not explain why they rose and took. It could not be the whole or the main account of that day's angling; for the rise and the take continued when the sun was low, and setting, and set.

The day-long rise and take were not due to the trout's appetite, nor to anything special in the artificial fly, nor to any hatch of natural fly, nor to the state of the water, nor to wind and weather; they were not due to anything visible or tangible in the trout or their environment. We are bound therefore, it would seem, to refer it to a mass impulse, which would come under the heading 'phychological factor', as explained above. The familiar, brief daily rise probably comes under the same heading; but on the day in question for some unknown reason the rise was unusually vigorous and long sustained.

Collective or mass impulses occur in human society. Thought-transference between individuals or members of a small group takes place; and thought transference is often the precursor of the common impulse. In time of war or national tension telepathic communication of feeling and desire occurs, and shows in panics, triumphs and other stirrings of the general mind and will. In all such phenomena the ordinary modes of individual apprehension are temporarily suspended or transcended, and are superseded by broader currents of thought and will.

Collective or mass impulses occur in nature over a wide field; the most obvious forms are mass movements, like migrations, and the most significant forms are those, like the spawning impulse, that are exhibitions of purpose and the mass mind. The angler says to himself, 'The sea trout will be up at the end of the month. I must have my tackle ready, and plans laid.' He is counting on the mass impulse and the mass mind. The migration of migrant fish has parallels in widely different fields. We find it among birds, crabs, locusts and lemmings. The most marvellous of all is the migration of eels. Eels leave their home in the Saragossa Sea and make an incredible Odyssey from the ocean through our seas into our rivers and streams and streamlets and canals. Why do they do it, and how are they taught? To call it a mechanical reaction is to pile Pelion on Ossa, all to no purpose. Who or what gives the signal for their return journey, and guides it? On some dark, wet, autumn night the homing instinct grips the eels; they cross damp meadows, and slip silently downstream from river to sea, and then from sea to ocean, and thus home again to the Saragossa Sea, to mate and die. It were incredible but that it is scientific fact. It were impossible, but for the psychological factor in the pattern of sub-human life.

In the beehive the migration impulse appears at swarming time; but the whole life of bees seems conditioned by collective impulse and ruled by the psychological factor. Many have written well about the bee; but for poetic insight and philosophical penetration Virgil's account in his fourth *Georgic* of 'the heavenly gift of ethereal honey' stands apart. Virgil kept bees and studied them, and speaks as if he loved them, not merely as a theme for his magic poetry, but as a marvellous spectacle (*admiranda spectacula*); and it is a marvellous spectacle to see a new swarm filing into their new quarters, like a Guards' battalion under orders, the many working as one, under the common impulse to live together under rule, and build, repair and work for one another and for posterity.

The peculiarity of the rise on the King's River on the 21st of June, 1939, was its long continuance. I have recorded the facts, but do not pretend to offer a full explanation. The clear sky, the bright sun and the keen air may have contributed; atomic energy, for all I know, may have contributed, of that curious pull postulated by the 'sol-lunar' theory. We may call it a form of midsummer madness, perhaps touched off by seasonal changes in the trout's physique. Whatever the impulse was, it was communicated to a large number of trout for a long time in no ordinary way. I have known things like it on the western lakes, but never on the same scale, or for so long a period. Whatever may have been the full explanation, part of it, I feel sure, was non-mechanical; something remarkable of a psychological nature occurred in the trout world in that stretch of water; their responses were quickened; their inhibitions were relaxed, and my best day on the river was the result.

Sir Cranley Onslow

Fishing is Different

T here are many pursuits that can take you to beautiful places, and many sports where success can give you great satisfaction. But in one all-important respect angling is unique. It is the only sport where failure is not necessarily your fault.

At cricket you can always be out first ball. In football you can miss an open goal. On the golf course you may take ninety strokes for the first nine holes. With your gun you can miss clay after clay. No success, no excuse.

Fishing is different.

If the fish will not take, it may be because the day is too hot – or too cold. The water may be too high or too low. The sun may be too bright, or the wind too strong. Or the fish – if they are there at all – may just not feel like feeding.

None of these things can possibly be your fault. Success is not yours to command, so failure is no shame. So you have no need to worry whether you catch a fish or not. You are free to enjoy the beauty of your surroundings, the delight of being in the open air.

Never forget: there is much more to fishing than just catching fish.

Billee Chapman Pincher

Nature Watch

No other sport brings its participants into such close contact with the natural world as fishing does. Over the years it has opened my eyes to so much of which I was previously unaware, even though I had been brought up in the Norfolk countryside when it was much more unspoiled than it is today. In addition, others have told me about their observations on the riverside. Some of their stories are of the unexpected, even the mysterious, others are of nature's rapacity, while most are of simple, sometimes earthy, delights.

Typical of the first category is the story – a literal tail of the unexpected – supplied by Don Macer-Wright of Dean Hall at Little Dean, in Gloucestershire, whose company I enjoyed when he looked after the stretch of the Kennet where I fish.

> I was recently on the banks of the Wye at a favourite and hidden spot where the river winds along the edge of the Forest of Dean, and I was privy to an extraordinary collection of natural events which, in the southern Britain of the 1990s, seem totally implausible. While contemplating the scene before me and wondering where else one could hear the calls of ravens, buzzards and a peregrine falcon all at the same time, I suddenly noticed a most peculiar tail. Below me, in the water, a tangle of willow caused a slack and, at the head of it, I could see a motionless tail pointing upstream in the oddest position, facing the current. Suddenly, a large old fallow buck intruded itself into my vision and, to my astonishment, disturbed an otter, which slid down the bank into the tangled willow. At that moment the tail I had spotted shot out of the cover to reveal a huge pike, over 25 pounds, with a half-swallowed fish in its jaws. The pike made an enormous swirl and disturbed the buck which, sensing me then, made off into the woodland thicket. The whole experience had happened in the space of a few seconds.

The kingfisher features regularly in the stories I have come across, but nowhere more delightfully than in that provided by Mr George Willis, a builder from Feltham.

I had been carp fishing all night, using two rods in Bedfont Lake, a former gravel pit in Middlesex. As usual I was sitting on a bed-chair under a big umbrella. When dawn broke, the morning was fine. I poured a cup of coffee and was rolling a cigarette when a kingfisher came and settled on the right-hand rod. This had happened to me several times before in my long hours of carp fishing. I froze to watch it as it dived from the rod to catch a small fish, which it killed by dashing it against the carbon-fibre rod before swallowing it. It did this twice more and then became interested in the line, which was hanging limp. It reached over, took the line in its beak and set off the little bite-alarm. This startled it but did not make it fly. I noticed later that its beak had been so sharp that it had kinked the nylon line.

The bird then flew off about 15 yards and settled on a piece of concrete about 5 feet above the water, so I continued to watch its antics. It dived and flew back with another fish, which it killed, but this time instead of swallowing it the bird shuffled to the edge of the concrete and dropped it into the water. The fish sank and the kingfisher dived again to retrieve it. Knowing that it was already dead, the bird did not dash the fish against the concrete but immediately dropped it back into the water. This performance was repeated five or six times and I was left in no doubt that either the kingfisher was getting in some diving practice or if was simply enjoying itself playing with the fish. I did not catch a carp, so the bird provided the highlight of the outing.

The brief experience recorded in the diary of Colin Farnell, a fellow member of my trout syndicate, was probably rarer in ornithological terms.

In June 1973, while I was standing very still holding my split-cane fly rod waiting for a fish to rise, a reed bunting perched on the end of it.

Steven Penney, head river keeper to the Duke of Wellington at Stratfield Saye, witnessed some surprising bird behaviour on a rather larger scale.

While fishing the Kennet with a friend we both saw a heron fly off with a full-grown tufted duck in its bill. Astonished that it could carry such a load, we did all we could to frighten it into dropping the duck, which was still alive because we could see its legs moving, but we had no success. It was November so the heron was not taking it back to a nest to feed its young and was, I suppose, taking it to feed off it itself. While herons regularly take ducklings nobody I have met has seen or heard of anything like this behaviour. However, I have seen two ducks, one of them a full-grown mallard, with heron stab wounds.

As an example of greedy predation, the story given to be by Andrew Hicks would be hard to better.

> I was beside the lake at Elnham House in Norfolk, talking to friends, when we noticed a fully grown mute swan with its head under water and its tail up as though feeding on the bottom. After a while one of us remarked that the swan's head had been submerged for rather a long time. When it remained tail up for several more minutes, we went to investigate. We managed to pull it into the side without a struggle and were astonished to find that its head was firmly clamped inside the jaws of a large pike. Both creatures were dead. The swan had drowned because the pike, which weighed 12 pounds, had been too heavy for it to heave out of the water. The pike had been unable to breathe because the swan's head and beak were so far down its throat that its gills could not function, while its backward-pointing teeth had made regurgitation impossible.
>
> Clearly the pike had seen the head and neck of the swan as manageable prey but the body of what is the world's heaviest flying bird had been too much for it.

Of course, what the angler sees or does not see depends on the intensity of his concentration on the task in hand. If this is excessive he can completely miss the unexpected, as Bill Rushmer, a well-known coarse fisherman of Ashford in Middlesex, records – with a touch of regret, I suspect.

> I was fishing the Little Pond at Frensham in Surrey with a few friends very early one summer morning in 1987. We had arrived at about 4 a.m. to try for some of the big tench there. I had not been fishing long, watching my waggler float with great intensity, when I was into a good fish and called for my net, which was a few yards away because I had moved a short distance on hooking the fish. Although I could hear my friends close nobody came to my assistance. All I could hear was a lot of clicking as though they were practising with the cameras which every coarse angler takes with him to photograph any specimen fish before returning them to the water. Eventually, I had to feel for the net myself and landed the tench, a beauty weighing 6 pounds 5 ounces. 'Thank you all very much,' I shouted. Again there was no response. By the time I had rebaited they were prepared to tell me what had been happening. While I had been busily engaged, an attractive young girl who had preceded us to the lake for a pre-breakfast swim, had emerged from the water. She was stark naked and, as her car and clothes were on the other side of us, she simply strode past, not a bit abashed, while my colleagues made the most of the situation with their cameras. She had been within fifteen yards of my back and I never got a glimpse of her. In fact, I was not sure that I believed their story until, a few days later, I saw their photographs.

Mary M. Pratt

Can Fish Communicate?

A simple answer to this question is 'yes'. They do it, however, in a way quite different from and much simpler than our complex system of spoken and written language.

Communication amongst fish probably consists of the exchange of simple sets of signals which contain information about potential danger or about aggressive or amorous intentions. The sending out of the signals and the response given to them by the receiver are all part of inherited patterns of behaviour. When fish communicate they are behaving instinctively, triggered off by particular stimuli or a particular set of circumstances.

Evidence that fish use their sense of smell in communicating with each other comes from some experiments with minnows in which all the members of a shoal showed a strong fright and escape reaction when a damaged fish was placed in their midst. Following this up it was discovered that certain 'alarm' substances are released from damaged tissue and that other fish when stimulated by these, take fright and swim away. This is a way in which an injured fish can say 'I'm being attacked – swim for your lives!'

Communication as a prelude to mating has been studied extensively in sticklebacks. Here the swollen shape of the female's belly is the signal which tells the male that the time is ripe for eggs to be laid and for him to chase the female through the nest and fertilise them. This is an example of visual communication – a very simple sort of sign language.

Many fish can produce sounds – indeed fishermen (mainly of the marine variety) have been known to listen for the presence of fish. There is little space here to go into the fascinating details of this, but the following examples show some of the ways that sounds can be produced. Most teleost fishes possess opposing sets of teeth in the throat region and these can be rubbed against each other to produce a grating sound. A fish which is rather expert at this is one splendidly named the white grunt. Several species of catfish produce sounds by the movements of fins and some, for example the sea horse, can rub together adjacent bones in the body to produce some sort of coarse noise. The swim-bladder is also used, usually as a resonator, but sometimes actually as a drum – the trigger fish is reputed to beat its pectoral fins against the region of the body wall covering the swim-bladder. In fish where the swim-bladder opens into the oesophagus gurgling noises can be made by the expulsion of air – a sort of burping, to put is less politely. What such sounds mean, if anything, to other fish is a wide open question for future research to answer. The examples given are of fish species which are not amongst our common freshwater fishes. It may well turn out though that some of our more familiar fish have a means of simple sound communication. The obvious group to start investigating would be the carp family since carp have a more highly developed auditory system than other species.

The ability to produce a fairly strong electric field is peculiar to fish and many fish (again not the ones familiar to us) have sensory systems for the detection of electrical activity in the water. Again, about the importance of these to the fish, little is known but it is possible that they can use their electrical apparatus to signal danger or courtship intentions to one another.

We can conclude then that by virtue of their sense organs for picking up information, the ability to process that information in the nervous system and to make certain responses to certain situations, plus their capacity to learn from experience, fish are well able to cope with life in their aquatic environment. Though they appear to us to do remarkably intelligent things there is no need to think of explanations in human terms – fish have their own ways.

Arthur Ransome

Fishing in Books and Fishing in Fact

A succession of bad days and a library of fishing books have led me to the conclusion that there are two quite different kinds of angling and that the relation between the two is like that between Arcadia and normal country life. Fishing in print takes place in a golden age. If the sun shines there it shines not too brightly. A storm is deprived of all its wetting power. The wind, tamed and orderly, does not use casting lines for the making of fishermen's puzzles, but, if you are casting against it, separates like the Red Sea before the Israelites to let your flies slip through in Indian file and gossamer procession, and, if you cast with it, holds them suspended at any length you wish until you drop them, lighter than thistledown, to be engulfed upon the instant by 3-pounders that follow you about to play their part in the happy pastoral scene. In books, a rise is a rise, a gold, spotted, heraldic fish slashes head and tail in the air or takes your fly with quiet decorum, you tighten with a turn of the wrist, play him downstream, lead him down the central aisle through a congregation of other trout so intent upon a sermon, or the next paragraph of the book, that they notice him as little as well-behaved parishioners notice the noisy urchin being lead out by the churchwarden. They must not notice him, for in the next paragraph it is their turn to take the fly and find their way in a manner as orderly as a minuet to the safe haven of your basket. In books the fish and the weather know their parts. They are word-perfect, as the actors say. In books, so are you.

In books you observe, while you are setting up your rod, a flotilla of flies, sailing downstream like little goosewinged schooners. You catch one, plucking it from the stream as you would pluck a flower. In books there is no difficulty about that. You look at the fly and call it by its name. Then, in older books, you find in your dubbing bag a hare's ear, some hackles from a gamecock, some wool, some feathers from the starling's breast, and, in a single sentence, you make a fly, a little smaller than the original but otherwise exactly like it. In modern books, you open an aluminium box and find there, made by Cummins, or Hardy, or Farlow, the very fly you need. You put it on. Four simple words of one syllable each, so unlike the real life business of finding the eye with the gut, making one knot and then another, pulling two out in the process of making fast and finally breaking the gut in testing your handiwork by the gentlest tug. Then, of course, your gut straightens itself by magic and at the first cast you see the fly alight over the large trout that, quite undisturbed by your flycatching, is rising now and again, as if to remind you he is waiting upon your convenience in putting your tackle together. Everything goes right and if you miss a rise you will be given another chance and have him. You lunch on the bank when the rise is over and contemplate your beauties, fairer than any picture, as decorations in your airy sylvan parlour. You do not hang your flies in hawthorn bushes, or, if you do, the incident is made delightful by your finding there the complete, undamaged cast of some less fortunate fisherman. There are no wasps, or if there are they busy themselves in driving away a bull who might otherwise have annoyed you. There are no little boys. There are no other anglers until, just as you are taking your rod to pieces to go home, one who has had a day's fishing not in the books, an ordinary day's fishing, stops beside you, and before he has seen into your crammed basket, tells you that the river is out of order and that it is little wonder that the fish are taking nothing.

Writers of angling books must be men of weak memories upon whose callous brains only the most memorable events make sharp impression. They write at Christmas time, or between Christmas and the opening of the season, if they be trout fishermen, or in the months of April and May if they be fishermen for pike or roach. Only the most memorable moments of the past season are in their minds, and they sweeten their recollections with their hopes of the season that is to come. Opportunity lacks to test their good resolves. They are determined to have no bad habits by the waterside and so they have none in their studies. If the weather be unpropitious, it is all the more promising for the time of which they think, and if it be a perfect day as they look up from their desks, they add its perfection to the fishing that they are putting upon paper.

Of fishing in fact there is hardly need to write. There is not a fly on the river. If there is, you cannot catch it. If you catch it you have nothing like it in your expensive collection. You miss rise after rise. You try smaller flies, get more rises and miss them too. You begin to put more force into your strike and presently break a hook in the mouth of a good fish, miss the next four rises from being too tender and lose your fly over the fifth. You notice a good fish under a big smooth stone on the opposite side of the river. Remembering the books, you cast so as to drop your fly on the stone, from which it is to fall, as an insect might and be engulfed by the monster. That smooth stone, even as you cast, cracks imperceptibly, receives your fly into the crack and holds it fast. You have to wade across to release it and as you wade disturb a much larger fish in a much easier place. The water gurgles in over your wading stockings. You have to pull for a break and lose the last specimen you have of the fly that has been getting all the rises. At last you hook a fish decidedly under size, so badly that you have to kill him, at which moment the water-bailiff strolls up and you have to explain to him. He pretends to believe you and asks to see the rest of your catch. He then tells you that Mr X a little further down has been having a very good day, and suggests that you should put on the fly that you have just lost. Finally after fishing till dusk, you set off home. On the way, you take a cast, just for luck, in a place where you missed a good one, and get caught up in a tree behind you. You break your cast, strain the middle joint of your rod in taking it to pieces, find that you left the stoppers at the place where you put the rod up, it being now too dark to look for them, tell yourself that after all stoppers do not matter, and in taking off your waders learn that they have been torn by a bramble. In all this I have said nothing about the weather. Suffice it that at starting out you have told your wife that it is too good a fishing day to miss.

Donald V. Roberts

An Angry Birth

n the time when the mountains still steamed from the womb and only rivers dampened the earth, there roamed a gigantic silver-maned grizzly. This irascible old bear, a creature as ancient as rounded granite, delighted in his vast territorial reign.

During one of his many autumn odysseys down the sunset side of the Cascades, he felt a hunger as wide and as empty as the sky. He stopped at a coastal river too young to have a name and with one paw scooped out all of the fish. He engorged lustily on the squirming meal. Feeling heavy and drowsy, Grizzly settled back on a grassy bank in the sun and slumbered while his long, black, splendid tail languished, cooling in the river current.

Meanwhile, the barnacle-covered grandmother of all brown trout returned from feeding at sea to discover that entire generations of her offspring had disappeared. Brown Trout peered up through the river froth and swam into the shadow of the fat bear. She measured the magnificent tail dangling in the river and lunged forward with her serrated jaws spread wide for slashing. Brown Trout chopped off the gorgeous tail where it joined Grizzly's broad hindquarters. Grizzly awoke with a bawl that made entire groves of aspen quake forever.

Grizzly regarded his pruned backside, first with disbelief, then with awful, mounting rage as his reason for vanity sank into an emerald pool. Brown Trout fled for her life as the sympathetic river roared with laughter. Grizzly followed, swiping and biting at the sinuous river which aided Brown Trout's wild flight. Finally, in clumsy, homicidal desperation and to prevent Brown Trout from ever going to sea again, he ripped the river loose from the earth and tied it into a colossal knot. The river, now tied like a tongue, never spoke again, except in sighs, and the water grew still and deep.

Grizzly, still unsatisfied with his revenge, pursued Brown Trout in the dark, tranquil water. Having nowhere to escape from the lunging bear, she leaped from river to river across the entire land. Grizzly tied knots in rivers until his paws grew numb, and upon seeing the sun blaze across a strange sea, he gave up the chase to wander back to his mountain home. Brown Trout became the meanest and most cautious of all fish to haunt the water recesses.

Today there lies a vast array of sighing lakes, shimmering like opals inset on the breastplate of the continent.

(Translated from carvings by Hygelac of the Weider-Geats upon barsalt of the Columbia Escarpment, 12 AD.)

Nick Faldo

Postscript

As a keen fisherman myself, I was delighted when Doug Hulme asked me to lend my support to the Second Chance charity. I grab every opportunity I can to 'get away from it all' by going fishing and have been lucky enough to experience some wonderful days fishing in different places around the world between golf tournaments. For all of you who, like me, enjoy a day's fishing, why not try and see if you can help raise money for these very special children while taking part in a sport you love?